CRITICAL PRAISE FOR INDIAN CREEK CHRONICLES

"*Indian Creek Chronicles* is a love song to Idaho's Selway-Bitterroot wilderness, to the relationship between self and solitude, to the wildness of the land and the landscape of the heart. Like all the best love songs it is honest, lyrical, and full of a kind of an ineffable wonder. Anyone who has ever loved a place truly will surely love this book."
—Pam Houston, author of *Cowboys Are My Weakness*

"Pete Fromm is an honest, objective, and impeccably focused observer of the natural world, and a superb writer to boot. His sentences have the impact of an ax cleaving chunks of frozen stovewood, and *Indian Creek Chronicles* is as satisfying as ten cords freshly split and stacked and ready for winter."
—Jerry Dennis, author of *A Place on The Water*

"*Indian Creek Chronicles* is a swift absorbing tale....He [Pete Fromm] has made me shake out my heavy winter sleeping bags with renewed enthusiasm."
—John Husar, *The Chicago Tribune*

"This retelling of Fromm's foray into the wild is strangely compelling....It was a long haul for Fromm, a brute circumstance, full of tribulation. But he survived to write this fresh-faced account. Bully for him."
—*Kirkus Reviews*

"...And for those of us who are probably never going to get around to acting out our own fantasy of a winter snowbound in a lonely cabin in the mountains, Pete Fromm's is a wonderful adventure to adopt."
—*Bozeman Daily Chronicle*

"Superbly crafted and a compelling read."
—*Sports Afield*

"I loved Pete Fromm's *Indian Creek Chronicles*. His account of his transformation from a callow kid to a seasoned woodsman is hilarious, touching, and unique."
—Stephen Bodio

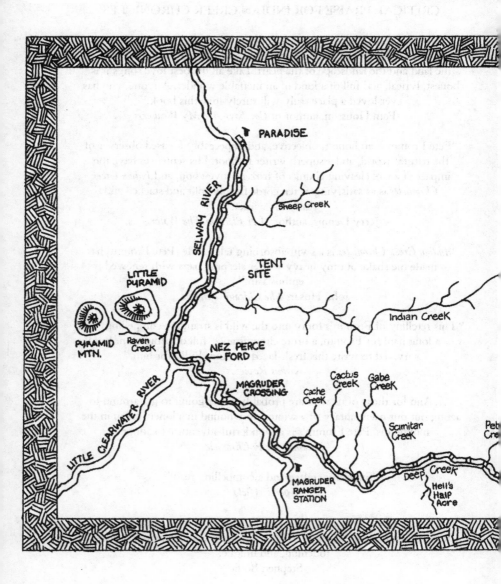

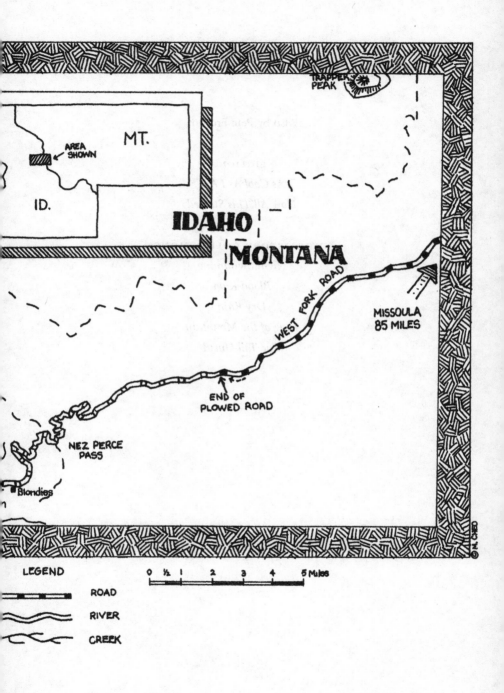

TRAPPER PEAK

MT.

AREA SHOWN

ID.

IDAHO
MONTANA

WEST FORK ROAD

MISSOULA
85 MILES

END OF
PLOWED ROAD

NEZ PERCE
PASS

Blondies

LEGEND

0 ½ 1   2   3   4   5 Miles

━━━━━━━ ROAD

〜〜〜 RIVER

〜〜〜 CREEK

Also by Pete Fromm

FICTION
As Cool As I Am
How All This Started

SHORT STORY COLLECTIONS
Night Swimming
Blood Knot
Dry Rain
King of the Mountain
The Tall Uncut

INDIAN CREEK CHRONICLES

PETE FROMM

Picador

New York

To Ellen for the books, and Big Dan and Paul for trying, and finally to Radar, my connection to the world.

Acknowledgments
A condensed version of the final several chapters, "Spring Runoff," was a winner of the 1991 *Sierra* Nature-Writing Contest, appearing in that magazine's November 1991 issue.

Chapter Nine was originally published in slightly different form under the title "To Be a Mountain Man," in the November 1992 issue of *Gray's Sporting Journal*.

The author would like to thank John and Susan Daniel and Ruth McLaughlin for their help with the manuscript.

www.picadorusa.com

Picador® is a U.S. registered trademark and is used by St. Martin's Press under license from Pan Books Limited.

For information on Picador Reading Group Guides, as well as ordering, please contact the Trade Marketing department at St. Martin's Press.
Phone: 1-800-221-7945 extension 763
Fax: 212-677-7456
E-mail: trademarketing@stmartins.com

Library of Congress Cataloging-in-Publication Data

Fromm, Pete.
    Indian Creek chronicles / Pete Fromm.
        p. cm.
    ISBN 0-312-42272-5
    1. Fromm, Pete, 1958– —Homes and haunts—Selway—Bitterroot Wilderness (Idaho and Mont.) 2. Outdoor life—Selway—Bitterroot Wilderness (Idaho and Mont.) 3. Selway—Bitterroot Wilderness (Idaho and Mont.)—Biography. 4. Authors, American—20th century—Biography. I. Title.

[PS3556.R5942Z469 1994]
818'.5403—dc20
[B]   94-12910
                                                                       CIP

First published in the United States by Lyons & Burford, Publishers

20 19 18

1

Once the game wardens left, the little tent we'd set up seemed even smaller. I stood in front of it, shivering at a gust I thought I felt running across my neck. Could this really be my home now? My home for the next seven months? For the entire winter? Alone? I glanced up at the river canyon's steep, dark walls, already cutting off the mid-afternoon sun. Nothing lay beyond those walls of stone and tree but more of the Selway-Bitterroot Wilderness. I was alone, in its very heart.

The shadow of the canyon's wall fell over me and I hurried away from it, into the sunlight remaining in the meadow. My steps rustled through the knee high grass and the breeze soughed through the towering firs and cedars hemming the small opening. The river's whispering rush ran through it all, creating an insistent quiet that folded around me like a shroud.

I stopped at the phone pole the warden had said would link me to the outside. Yesterday we'd discovered the phone didn't work. I picked it up anyway, listening to its blank silence, the voice of the rest of the world. With the receiver still against my ear I turned and looked back at the shadowed tent, far enough away now for perspective.

The canvas walls closed off an area fourteen by sixteen feet. The wardens had told me that, bragging it up, making it sound spacious.

On the phone, sitting at a college swimming pool, when I'd been accepting this job, it had sounded palatial.

Now I hung up the empty phone and walked back to the tent. Pulling the door flap aside I stepped in, out of the wilderness. A pile of boxes and bags—all my possessions and supplies for seven months—stood in the center of the floor, greatly reducing the space in the tent. I remembered the way, only yesterday, those boxes and bags had filled my dorm room, and the way my roommate and I had carved trails through them to get around.

I sat down on the pile and Boone, the little rat-like dog my roommate had given me, sat on my foot. She had been weaned too early for this and didn't want anything to do with anything unless she was within a foot or two of my leg. I took a big, shaky breath and scratched her drooping ears, whispering, "It's beautiful here, isn't it, Boone?" But instead of being able to conjure up any excitement for seven months of solitude, I sat and petted her warm head, wondering how in the world I'd wound up here.

I thought of that first call to the warden, from the swimming pool where I'd first heard of this job, and I realized that swimming had started me toward this dark, lonely tent long before I ever could have guessed.

The very first step on the long trail here could well have been the one my brother missed on a stairway in Milwaukee, four years earlier. Paul, my twin, the high school swimming star, had broken his leg by the time he reached the bottom of those stairs, ending his swimming that season, but starting mine.

The coach was on me first thing the next morning. "You Fromm's twin?" he wanted to know.

Though we didn't look a bit alike, I couldn't see any point in lying.

"Good. Practice starts at 3:30. See you there."

"I don't swim," I said.

"You're Paul's twin, right?"

When I didn't bother answering again he said, "3:30," and walked out the door.

When the last bell rang that afternoon I started home, only swerving into the pool building at the last possible moment. Until I was inside, the reek of chlorine engulfing me, I'd never thought of going. Unwittingly, I'd made the first in a series of completely unconsidered decisions leading to the tent.

I struggled through twenty laps and when everyone stopped I thought it was over. Nobody could possibly swim another stroke. But the coach assigned the next set and I flailed away with the rest of them. Anything else would have been giving up. Though this wasn't my world, I wasn't about to face that kind of shame.

This was junior year. The year of college selections. But the world of swimming swept me up and I couldn't have thought less about college. By senior year even my lunches were spent at the pool, making up for lost time, churning the water back and forth alone, with just the coach walking alongside me on the deck, shouting encouragement. With that in my ears and the searing oxygen debt in my lungs I forged new worlds for myself in my head—world records, the Olympics, Mark Spitz's seven golds around my neck—laying the foundation for a life of daydreaming. Well suited to solitude.

Toward the end of my senior year I spent more and more time deflecting my parents' questions about college until the day a sheet of paper slipped from a friend's pile of college catalogs. A bighorn sheep stood boldly atop the page, a stirring symbol of wildness and freedom. Beneath it were the obscure words *Wildlife Biology* and *University of Montana*.

For years my family had taken summer camping trips, starting with a trailer, progressing through family-sized canvas tents, and finally to canoe trips and even a backpacking trip or two. The less civilized the better, I thought, and I'd often have the family drop me off as they drove to guided nature walks. I preferred exploring alone, seeing what there was to see without some guide telling me what to look at, without becoming part of what I saw as a crowd of ignorant city dwellers. Mooching, my father called it. Mooching around.

I'd never heard of wildlife biology, but it sounded pretty much like professional mooching. In the second of a series of decisions without thought, I sent out just one college application.

My knowledge of western geography was sketchy and I didn't know how to pronounce the word *Missoula*, but three months later I landed there, a wildlife biology major. And though I didn't know it yet, the tent site on the Selway River was only eighty miles away, as the crow flies.

By the end of my first day in Missoula I'd joined the swim team. I'd felt adventurous coming to this empty state alone, but now I felt lost, and I fell gratefully into the discipline of the workouts. By winter quarter I had a scholarship, an official reason to be in Montana.

For the next two years my days started with an exhausted shuffle to the pool in the dark and ended with an even more worn-out trudge back from the pool in the early night of winter. I was in Montana, though for all I saw of it, it could have been anywhere else in the world. But the last meet was in March, and spring was all my own.

During my second year in Montana my roommate was a guy from Ohio, Jeff Rader, a hunter. He was older by a few years and, while I spent my summers lifeguarding at a Wisconsin country club, he was a seasonal ranger for the National Park Service. While I had goggles and Speedos, he had rifles and shotguns. And he had a car, a battered green station wagon he called the Deerslayer. That spring, released from the crushing exhaustion of the workouts, we began to explore the country around Missoula, and I began to realize what I'd been missing.

Rader was also a reader, something I'd never been, and he would whistle in awe at the things he read, or laugh so hard I finally began picking up the books he finished. He was working through the library's entire collection of mountain man stories. In Montana, that's a big collection. Jim Beckworth's ridiculous tall tales of becoming a Crow chief and single-handedly whipping every other tribe in the Northwest, and *Lord Grizzly*, with Hugh Glass's monumental crawl after a grizzly mauling, lying in streams to let the minnows lip the maggots out of his back, began to be the things I'd dream about. I read of the mountain man's all-purpose Green River knife, and his muzzle-loading Hawken rifles. Jim Bridger, Liver-Eating Johnson, Jedediah Smith, John Colter all became names I lived with more than those of my classmates. When I read A.B. Guthrie's *The Big Sky* I walked around in a daze, the next Boone Caudill, waiting to explode.

But even through the haze of romance I could still, at times, read between the lines. I'd winter camped, not with buffalo robes and tepees, but with what modern technology had to offer. I'd backpacked until I thought I would drop and I'd wished for escalators instead of switchbacks. I asked Rader if he didn't think all the stuff those guys went through wasn't, at the time, the biggest pain in the ass they could've imagined.

"Sure," he said. "But that always makes the best stories afterwards. When they were geezers I bet it's all they ever talked about. Like guys who've been in wars."

I was nineteen and that made sense. And, worst of all, I came to the awful realization that I had no experiences like that, nothing that would make a story worth telling anyone, not when I was a geezer, not even right now. Though my questions still nagged from time to time, I shoved them away. They seemed vaguely traitorous, even weak. I didn't ask about it again. Instead I picked up the next book. Pretty soon I was making a pair of knee-high moccasins for myself, in the Flathead style, though secretly I pretended they were Blackfeet. Blackfeet were much tougher.

Over spring break Rader and I and his buddy Sponz and a few others piled into the Deerslayer and took a "rendezvous" trip down to the Tetons. We grilled chicken over an illegal fire and drank cheap whiskey the way the mountain men did in the books. We passed the bottle back and forth, swigging mountain-manfully. Later, when I tried to stand up, I pitched back down face first and couldn't walk again until the next morning, when I didn't much feel like it. The drinking described in the books began to seem impossible, but somehow I didn't extend that to any of the rest of their tales. I wore my moccasins the whole time and wished I'd been born a hundred and fifty years earlier, closer to the tent on the Selway than I ever could have imagined.

When I hit campus for my third year in the fall of 1978, I learned the swim team had been cut. I was furious with the school and my core classes in chemistry and calculus suddenly seemed farther from mooching than it was possible to get. What was I doing taking stuff like this?

To fill the sudden rush of free time I worked more and more hours at the pool and I put the finishing touches on a rifle kit I'd bought the spring before: a half-stock Hawken, .54 caliber. True mountain man stuff. I'd bought it though I had never owned a gun and I had no tools or experience to use in building it. Before I'd met Rader I'd never even seen a gun.

Toward the end of that September, a few days before I turned twenty, a girl who'd been on our spring rendezvous to the Tetons walked up to my lifeguard chair for a chat. She smiled and I felt like I was at the country club again, flirting with girls in suits like sheer second skins, and I knew this wasn't the way real mountain men acted. That summer had been my first away from home, working for the National Park Service at Lake Mead, Nevada, but even there I worked as a lifeguard, embarrassed I had no skills a real ranger needed.

The girl had spent the summer with a friend cooking at a wilderness lodge in Idaho. She was from New Jersey originally and she told me about the cooking and the hiking, Indian place names like Nez Perce Pass rolling off her Jersey twang. I'd read all about the Nez Perce. Chief Joseph. "I will fight no more forever." I was an expert. And here I sat in a Speedo, listening to a Jersey girl tell me about the mountains she'd lived in. The mountains I'd only read about.

I was barely listening when she told about her friend and the game warden they'd met in Idaho. Her friend had taken a job with the Idaho Fish and Game, she told me, one that would mean spending a winter in the mountains alone. Something to do with salmon eggs.

I was listening now. In the middle of the wilderness. Alone. Like a mountain man. She said she thought it sounded pretty cool, but her friend had hooked up with some guy and now it didn't sound so cool to her. After all, it was seven months alone. Just that day she'd called the warden and backed out. "Boy, was the warden pissed," she told me. She'd left him with two weeks to find somebody to spend seven months alone in the wilderness. Those people didn't grow on trees, she said, and the whole expensive project was hanging in the balance.

She gave me the name and number of the warden and I called him from the pool. Like a mountain man would have. Resourceful. Leaping at opportunity before it slipped away. Before thought could enter into the equation.

Although I could hear how excited the warden was to have this call drop on him from the blue, he was careful to explain just what the job entailed. In fact, he said he wouldn't let me accept before he went through a list of the conditions. He didn't want anybody accepting it on some romantic whim, only to back out on him again. He actually used that word—*romance*. I'm sure he hadn't intended it, but he hooked me with just that one word.

"You'll be living in a canvas wall tent at the junction of the Selway River and Indian Creek," he told me. "Right in the middle of the Selway-Bitterroot Wilderness Area." I didn't know what a wall tent was, but I kept quiet. "It's just up from Paradise Guard Station. You know where that is?"

"No."

"It's where all the floaters put in," he said, pausing before going on. I'd never floated anything.

From mid-October to mid-June I would be responsible for two and a half million salmon eggs planted in a channel between the two streams. The closest plowed road was forty miles away; the closest person, sixty. If I was interested, he said, he could only give me two weeks to get ready.

I was hearing less and less of what he had to say. Everything sounded perfect. I'd finally find out about this mountain man stuff. Romance or real? Pain in the ass or glorious freedom? And, no matter what I discovered, I was sure it would be something I could tell about later, a story all my own.

I told the warden it sounded good, all of it. If I'd been listening more carefully, I could have probably heard him shaking his head.

"Don't you want to know how much it pays?" he asked.

I said of course I did, though I hadn't thought of that. He said, "Two hundred dollars a month."

"OK," I said. This was too good to be true. Getting paid too.

He told me to think about it and give him another call tomorrow. "No problem," I said. A formality.

I'd already accepted.

2

I mmediately after hanging up with the warden I called my parents. They weren't going to be too keen about my dropping out, but at first they were too busy asking other questions to get around to that. Most of their questions were ones I probably should have thought to ask the warden myself, such as: How would I communicate?

I told them I'd probably have a radio or something.

"How will you stay warm?"

"I guess it's a big tent. He said there was a wood stove."

"What if you cut your foot off with an ax? How will you get help?"

"I guess I'll use the radio," I said, and they said, "If you have one." I wondered who they thought could be lame enough to cut their foot off with an ax.

I wasn't reassuring them, but I thought of Hugh Glass crawling some ungodly distance, hundreds and hundreds of miles, after being chewed up and spit out by a grizzly bear. I mentioned that to them. "If things get real ugly," I said, "it's only forty miles. I could crawl that if I had to." That didn't reassure them at all.

My mother grew more and more logical, and I more and more defensive, throwing out things like, "This kind of experience will look really good. It's impossible to get any job in wildlife biology without a bunch of experience." My mother didn't think experience as a lunatic would help with anything.

"What about school?" she asked.

"It's only been going a week. I can drop out no problem."

There was silence then—none of their six kids had ever dropped out of anything. "I can always go back next year," I said, trying to fill in the hole, though my classes had come to seem so ridiculous I was far from sure if I'd bother returning.

My father finally said something like, "Well, I suppose it's opportunities like this that you went to Montana for."

I agreed vehemently, though I'd never really had any idea why I went to Montana.

My mother, on the bedroom phone, started to protest, but my dad interrupted long enough for me to hang up before things got worse. I stared at the phone in the office of the Grizzly Pool. Cut my foot off with an ax! What kind of a gimp did they think I was?

Rader would know how great this was. I changed as quickly as I could and ran across the green lawns of campus to tell him.

"Seven months?" he asked. "Without seeing anybody?"

I nodded, but added, "I guess they'll snowmobile in now and then. Bring me mail and stuff." I was reluctant to admit that. Seven months without any contact sounded a lot more mountain mannish.

"You're nuts," he said, but he was excited about it. He thought it'd be a great experience, though he wouldn't do it for anything. At the same time that made me think a little more about what exactly I'd agreed to do, it also made it all the more attractive. This wasn't something any idiot would do. This took a special breed.

Rader was considerably less swayed by romance than I was and he asked his own list of questions. How was I going to get into the middle of the wilderness?

There was a road into it, I admitted. "Some sort of corridor, he called it. It usually gets snowed shut by the end of October, beginning of November."

"So you don't have to horsepack all your stuff?"

I had to confess that I could bring it all in with the Fish and

Game pickup truck.

"So you got to get all your gear together? What about food?"

"I have to get it all before they come to pick me up."

"How long do you have?"

"Couple of weeks."

He whistled again, the same way he did when he read about some fantastic mountain man feat.

"They're paying for all your food?" he asked.

I shook my head. "I am, I guess. He didn't say anything about that."

"What about your scholarship?"

I hadn't thought of that. While Rader had scraped together his last dollars for tuition I'd walked out of registration with a check for five hundred dollars. "I guess I'll probably lose that."

He asked how much I made off my scholarship and I told him. He was never a miracle worker in math, so it was a minute before he said, "So you're giving up fifteen hundred bucks of scholarship for fourteen hundred bucks of pay."

I nodded.

"Well at least they're letting you pay for all your own food."

I nodded a little less certainly, not having thought about it quite like that.

"I wonder how much rent they'll charge for the tent."

"He didn't say anything about that," I told him. "They couldn't really make me pay rent."

Rader started to laugh and he reached out the window and snagged a couple of the stubby bottles of beer he had cooling on the sill. We knocked off the caps and he lifted his beer in a toast. "Fucking Fromm," he said, grinning and shaking his head. I glowed under his eloquence.

The next day I did business. Before I dropped out I tried everything I could to keep my scholarship. I finally got someone to admit that if I stayed enrolled my scholarship would stay intact. Rader and I sat back and wondered how that could be finagled. The next day I went into the unexplored liberal arts side of campus. I hooked up with a humanities professor, though I hadn't even known there was such a thing. When I walked out I was enrolled for the next three quarters, in an independent study course on journal writing. Three credits a quarter, Pass/No Pass, since it would be impossible to grade.

"Journal Writing!" we cackled. What in the world kind of a course was that? We agreed that I'd pulled a world class boondoggle.

The beers we cracked in celebration that first day uncorked a river of the stuff that flowed almost without stop for the next two weeks. Friends heard what I was doing and threw parties, or took me out on the town for a last taste of civilization. They took turns giving me send-offs, so no matter how bleary-eyed I grew there was always a fresh, eager face waiting to tie one on the next night.

All the shopping I had to do was done in the lulls of these festivities. I knew so little about what was needed I don't know if that hurt or not.

When I'd left Mom's table I'd moved straight to the college food service; I hadn't cooked anything but a hotdog or two in my life. Now seven months' worth of grocery shopping stared me down. Rader and I wandered the aisles of the bulk-rate food store in a quandary. I bought, as it turned out, enough rice for a few years and enough beans for decades. At the last instant I remembered to buy a percolator and a few pots and pans, things I'd never owned or used. And finally I added a hundred pounds of potatoes, saying I'd dig a food cache to keep them from freezing. I didn't really have any idea how to make such a thing, but the word *cache* was always creeping up in the mountain man books. It had a certain sound to it.

We bundled all the food into our tiny dorm room, forming an impressive pile, then set off for the fun stuff. Rader was convinced I wasn't going to eat beans all winter, but that I was going to become a skilled subsistence hunter. I'd never shot a thing in my life, but this too had a nice ring to it. We took the Deerslayer to the local sporting good store and I kissed my scholarship money goodbye.

I bought candles and axes and splitting wedges. I bought two pairs of snowshoes (one round and one long, though I wasn't sure what the difference was.) They were made from ash and rawhide, full of primitive, utilitarian beauty.

Wool pants were next; three pair, though two seemed like enough. I didn't want to be caught short in the wilderness.

Then the real fun began: the purchasing of all the mountain man accoutrements that would undoubtedly be essential. Though I had no idea how to work one, I bought traps—every mountain man needed traps. And Rader had trapped muskrats before in Ohio, and was willing to let me in on all his secrets.

Rader, in fact, pretty much took over at this stage, a kid run amuck in a candy store. A few days earlier we'd driven up to the mountains to fire my muzzle loader for the first time. I'd been nursing a screaming hangover and the boom and jar of the rifle had made my eyes water. But an impressive amount of thick blue smoke blossomed from the barrel with each shot and I was hooked. Rader was less impressed, saying I needed a real gun to survive. I mentioned that Liver-Eating Johnson hadn't needed any such thing, but in the gun department he talked me into buying a bolt-action .22. "For shooting rabbits and squirrels and stuff," he told me. "You hit one of those with your buffalo gun and you'll be looking for pieces for weeks."

When we got back to the dorm room I wrapped both rifles in the sheepskin and leather I'd bought to make myself another set of moccasins and a pair of mukluks.

As the day of leaving wound closer I added little things to the pile in our room, which by now we'd made trails through so we could get to our beds. Things like a buffalo horn I planned to turn into a true-blue powder horn. Only a few days before the wardens were due to arrive and drive me away I remembered matches and I added boxes and boxes of them. The big Ohio Blue Tips. The kind I'd always liked using on camping trips when I was a kid.

And finally I added a few books. I took *The Big Sky*—my bible—and things like *Foxfire* manuals and Bradford Angier's books on outdoor survival and an old Herter's pamphlet on wilderness recipes. Even after following Rader's lead into the whole mountain man morass, I wasn't much of a reader. I left for seven months alone with six books.

The weekend before the wardens came Rader dragged me out into the mountains for a hunting trip. It was opening day of big-game season, and he was going to get himself an elk.

I'd had a big night the night before and I was too tired to shop for food when we left. Anyway, I had my rifle and mountain men never had any grocery stores when they were in the woods.

By dusk, ten miles up some sorrowfully elkless trail near Lolo Peak, Rader and I made camp. My stomach was growling and twisting but I'd sat and watched Rader snack all day, too proud to admit that the mountain-man-to-be wanted a bite of that Snickers bar so bad he could taste it. Just before it got dark I shot a tree squirrel, one of the tiny red western ones. Nothing like the cat-size gray squirrels we had back home.

It was the first animal I'd ever killed and Rader showed me how to gut it. I was impressed how neat and clean the insides were, shiny and orderly, laid out exactly as our own. I figured Darwin must have had a similar peek into the workings of animals.

Rader showed me how to skin the squirrel, working the hide over its head like a sock. This would all be invaluable information, once I was locked into the hills running my trap line, saving pelts that I'd later transfer into a small fortune at Pacific Hide and Fur. I kept the squirrel's soft, furry tail.

As we sat around our campfire that night, sipping whiskey (I'd learned to sip, no matter what the books said), Rader ate one peanut butter sandwich after another, while I slowly turned the stick on which I'd impaled the squirrel's naked body. It grew blacker and tougher with every second over the flames and I finally ate it with feigned relish. My first kill. The inside was warm and the outside crusty, the meat tender as Naugahyde. It tasted of the pine we burned.

When Rader finally offered a peanut butter sandwich I hesitated until I was sure I would not be laughed at. Then I wolfed it down.

That night, while Rader snored on one side of the fire, I lay back in my bag and poked at the flames with a stick. We called them *roasting sticks* when we were little. I was starving and tired and cold, but I could not sleep. I wished I'd never seen the girl who'd come into the pool that afternoon. I thought of the pile of junk that had taken over our dorm room. Half of it I didn't know how to use, the other half I didn't want in the first place. How the hell were you supposed to cook a bean that was as hard as a diamond?

Worn down by the frenzied drinking with all my friends— friends I realized I wasn't going to be seeing again for a long time— those seven months finally began to seem like something real.

But the wardens were coming for me in two days and I'd had at least ten going away parties and there was no way in the world to get out of what I'd gotten myself into. No way. If the wardens had called saying the project was off and I wouldn't be able to go in after all, I would have danced a naked jig down Main Street. I closed my eyes and tried to force them to make that call. Things had snowballed far too long for me to back out on my own.

Rader and I hiked out the next day and I went straight to the food service. I met some friends there and early that afternoon the last of the going away parties started. I swung past my room later, to pick up Rader before we all went downtown.

He was sitting amongst all the boxes with Lorrie, a girl I'd gone out with my first year or so in Montana. She held a tiny, tiny puppy. It looked half shepherd, half rat, and all starved. "It's yours," Rader said. "You'd be crazy not to have a dog in there."

I looked at the scrawny little thing. "We picked her out at the pound," Rader said. "She's half husky, half shepherd. I waved a bunch of grouse tails at the whole litter and this one charged first." Rader was smiling, proud of himself.

I'd been drinking beer with the old swim team for several hours and I looked at Rader and the dog and Lorrie. I wondered when they had gotten friendly. She'd never liked him when we were going out.

"What are you going to call her?" Lorrie asked, holding the pup up for me.

"Boone," I said. After Boone Caudill. A natural.

Lorrie said, "It's a girl."

I nodded. "Boone."

Then I turned to Rader and told him we were all heading downtown. I set Boone down on the floor and she toddled back to Lorrie. "Did you get any dog food?" I asked, proud that I could think of such logistics.

"Uh uh."

"How much you suppose we'll need?"

"A few hundred pounds probably."

So we made one last shopping run, adding six fifty-pound bags of dog food to the pile.

When we dropped the dog food off I got a call informing me that my scholarship had been revoked. I had to be a full-time student, minimum twelve credits. I did some frenzied calling of my own, but it was hopeless and I watched the last of my money vanish. So much for boondoggles.

The party was on though, and I didn't bother taking the time to cross campus to drop out of my independent study course in journal writing. The notebooks were already packed.

That night became a blur. The party split up downtown and I didn't make it home until it was light out Monday morning.

The wardens had said they'd be in by eight or nine, since it was a long drive. They'd also said they'd bring maps, so I hadn't bought any of my own. About fifteen minutes before the wardens knocked on the door I realized for the first time that I really didn't have any idea where I was going.

3

The wardens were businesslike, emptying my dorm room of all its supplies much faster than I'd hoped. Soon there wasn't even an excuse left. My friends stood beside the Idaho Fish and Game trucks in the cool October sun, looking at me. Knowing there was nothing else to do, I shook hands all around, got a few kisses from the girls. I climbed into a truck then, with a warden, an older man, a total stranger. Boone crunched into my lap.

I waved as we pulled away from campus. Not four hours ago my going-away party had been in full, riotous swing, as it had been for the last two weeks, since my twentieth birthday, since I'd accepted this job, and I didn't feel very good. I managed to chat a little with the warden, but he smiled at my red eyes, saying they looked like road maps, that it must've been quite a send-off. I said it sure was, and though he was driving me deep into a place I had never been, and though he was going to leave me there for seven months, I was asleep against the passenger window before we left the string of fast food restaurants at the south end of Missoula.

I woke up in Darby, a place I had never heard of. While the warden filled the truck I bought a Coke at the gas station, wondering when I'd taste another. Though I rarely drank soda, suddenly I couldn't believe I hadn't brought any in with me. What else could I have overlooked? I read an old road map pinned to the wall and discovered we were already sixty-five miles south of Missoula.

We drove south out of Darby a few more miles, then turned off the highway onto another paved road. I realized I wouldn't be able to recognize the turn off, that I hadn't looked at the road signs. It seemed like a big mistake, though I couldn't see how that lack of information could hurt. I wouldn't be back out here until spring. But I didn't have any idea where we were and we dropped onto a bone-jarring stretch of dirt road that tried my stomach pretty hard; I couldn't tell if that was hangover, or the nervous, hopeless twisting of fear.

It was too hot in the truck and another stretch of smooth pavement followed. Without wanting to I fell asleep again.

When we hit the last stretch of dirt we were over the pass and sleep was impossible. I watched the narrow, jumbled river beside the truck and the steep, dark canyon walls that rose from its banks. It was a wet, dark looking place, with thicker, heavier vegetation than I was used to. The black sides of the river cut seemed to nearly snap shut over me.

We hit a big clearing half full of elk hunters' tents and the wardens pulled in. Indian Creek. Without talking much they pulled a bunch of lumber and plywood and the canvas tent from the back of one of the trucks and began cutting poles to set it up. After putting together a plywood floor, we hoisted the canvas on the ridge pole and I was left the job of tying off the guy line while they struggled to hold the tent upright. I ran the line around the tree they told me to and started looping it around itself in some sort of imitation of a knot. The warden, my boss, grunted, "A double half hitch would work best."

"A double what?"

We traded places and he tied the tent up. Then he took me aside and demonstrated a half hitch. "Haven't you ever messed around with rope?"

I shook my head and saw the wardens glance at each other. I tried harder not to appear stupid, but couldn't see why anyone would purposefully spend time "messing around with rope." I still felt terrible from the night before, and that had been tremendous fun. This, with these two old strangers, was not.

We unloaded my supplies next, stacking them into a pile inside. The warden pointed at the barrel of the twenty-two poking from the end of the rolled sheepskin. "You know you don't have any hunting licenses?"

I nodded.

The warden kicked at one of the sacks on the floor and a trickle of white beans spilled onto the plywood. "I guess I can hardly expect you to eat those all winter."

He glanced around the tent and at the other warden, then pointed at the rifle again. "When you use that, just be discreet about it. If Old Ironsides caught you shooting so much as a rabbit he'd tack your hide to a tree."

"Old who?" I asked.

He described the other warden for the district. "He's spent most of his career looking for some way he could arrest his mother," he said, and both the wardens laughed. "Odds are you'll never see him. But for all our sakes, be discreet. He'd probably try to arrest us for aiding and abetting."

"I was really just going to use it for plinking," I said, which was a lie. "I've never hunted," I added, which wasn't. He looked as if he believed me. After all, he knew I'd never once messed with rope.

We left the tent then and drove back upstream ten miles to a summer ranger station, Magruder, for the night.

In the morning the warden explained that they were going to leave the more battered truck with me over the winter. They both hopped into it and told me to go ahead and drive. Maybe they'd had a secret conversation. I killed the truck trying to get up the hill away from Magruder and they discovered I barely knew how to operate a manual transmission. They exchanged more worried looks and my boss began to explain the operations of a clutch. We lurched and bogged down for the next ten miles, but I made it without killing it until we reached the tent. I felt pretty good about that.

By the time they discovered I'd never run a chainsaw they weren't looking at me anymore. The boss handed me a saw file and told me I'd get the hang of sharpening. He didn't offer any instruction. I think they were trying not to get to know me, like veteran soldiers with a new recruit who probably won't survive long anyway.

I felt as if I'd just hatched or something, and though they were the only people I knew, it was so uncomfortable rubbing shoulders with their acres of knowledge I could hardly wait for them to leave. But when they said they'd be heading out by noon I wished there was some way to make them stay. At least one more day.

Back at Indian Creek my boss showed me the telephone stuck to a pole a hundred yards or so from my tent. It had a crank on the side I thought was pretty neat, like old time telephones. A single cable strung through the trees all the way from here to West Fork Ranger Station, forty miles away in Montana. He called it a land line and said to use it if there was any kind of emergency. "Crank the handle around," he said. "Two long and one short for the ranger station." As he explained it he demonstrated, but nothing happened over the phone.

"Tree must have dropped on the line," he said. Careful not to look me in the eyes, he said, "There's another one at Magruder. Maybe the break's between here and there."

They had a long drive back to Lewiston that day and were in an awful hurry to get out. I drove them to Magruder, where they'd left their truck and they stayed long enough to try that phone. It still worked and my boss said, "Great. Anything bad comes up this winter, use this one."

"If no trees fall on the line?" I asked, and the warden nodded. There was nothing out here but trees. I didn't ask how I was supposed to cover the ten miles between my tent and here once I'd cut my foot off with an ax. I was feeling pretty small, and maybe it was really more obvious than it seemed.

We stood around the two trucks in the pretty meadow in front of the old Magruder station and my boss went over clutch tricks with me again. Then he started talking about firewood. With the sun warm on us I wished he'd talk all day.

"We left you plenty of gas, and the saw. The gas is already mixed, you don't need to add oil. But don't forget the bar oil. You'll burn it up fast if you forget that." I kept nodding, as if I'd cut down whole forests before I ever met him.

"You'll probably need about seven cords of firewood," he told me. "Concentrate on that. You'll have to get it all in before the snow grounds your truck."

Though I didn't want to ask, it seemed important. "What's a cord?"

That seemed to be the one that broke their backs. They didn't even look at each other that time, and they sure didn't look at me. They'd been leaning against their open doors and they both got in and sat down. My boss rolled down his window. "A cord's how you measure firewood. It's a stack four feet deep, four feet tall, and eight feet long. You'll want at least seven of them. Ten would be nice if it gets to be a hard one. Nothing like dragging firewood through snow to ruin your day."

He reached out then and handed me a key to the ranger station and another for the gas pump. "You'll probably burn a tank just getting your firewood." Then he shook my hand suddenly and said, "Good luck," promising to try to get back in once before the road closed for good. As he let the clutch out he added, "You'll do fine," and they drove off.

I wasn't very sure of that myself, and when it took me three tries to get the truck up the hill without stalling, I was positive it was a lie.

4

I sat on the sloppy pile of supplies for a long time that first evening in my tent, stunned to actually find myself there. Had my stumble into swimming and a hunter roommate reading about mountain men really led to this? I kept scratching Boone's ears, remembering my first day ever in Montana, how the adventure had turned suddenly to loneliness and confusion. I'd retreated to the pool then, to the safe, familiar routine and discipline of workouts. I looked down at the pile of stuff beneath me, at the dingy gray light filtering through the canvas, and I knew there was no place to retreat to here, no pool to jump into, no coach who would shout instructions to me.

Finally I had to get out of the tent. I couldn't stand another second. I pushed myself up and walked down to the channel I was supposed to watch. The day was still warm, a notch in the mountains allowing the sun to touch the branches of cedars and firs for the last seconds before dusk. I reached out to touch the strands of yellow light filtering through the branches. It seemed I could nearly feel it. Not warmth, but as if each ray would have its own weight. Like it would be silky between my fingers. But it was not like that.

When the sun dipped below the mountains I climbed up the steep, open, southern face of Indian Ridge, just far enough to get out of the darkness of the canyon.

I sat down under a large ponderosa pine. Boone crawled into my lap. I thought of how dumb a name it was for a girl. I didn't feel too friendly toward A. B. Guthrie right then. It was *The Big Sky* and the rest of the mountain man books that had gotten me into this mess.

I watched the sun set again from up there, and had a view of one short twist of the river below me. A plane's contrail cut the air far, far above me and I wondered what the hell I was doing. I glanced upriver, to where Magruder was, with its phone. Ten miles away. I wondered again about crawling ten miles along that dark, damp river bottom after cutting my foot off with an ax. Nobody had ever seen Hugh Glass make his crawl, and he suddenly seemed as great a liar as Jim Beckworth.

Boone gave out on the return trip and I had to carry her the rest of the way. I slept that night in my sleeping bag, next to the pile of stuff I didn't have the heart to unpack. For a long time my throat was so tight and dry I thought I might suffocate if I drifted off to sleep. But sleep was a long time in coming that night, and my throat eased, more from exhaustion than any slacking of loneliness.

Although I woke beside the same unpacked pile of boxes, things didn't look so grim in the morning. I started a fire in the stove and the smell of the smoke and the chill in the air reminded me of every camping trip I'd ever been on. I fried a pair of eggs on top of the wood stove and ate them with pride. I was cooking. With that great success behind me I strolled down to get to work, Boone nipping at my heels.

My sole responsibility out here was the salmon channel: an eighty-yard-long ditch, six feet wide, filled with two feet of loose river stone. In early October the eggs had been brought from Idaho hatcheries and sifted down through the stones.

Salmon are born up here, or were anyway, before the Northwest dammed all their rivers. After wintering in the creeks they start a year-long trek to the ocean, over a thousand miles for these fish. Then, after three or four years in the Pacific, they return to where they were born, to spawn and die. Most don't make it of course, what with the dams and the fishing. This whole program was just to try to get enough for fishing. The wardens had explained all this to me. I was still only taking core classes in Missoula and while I was pretty knowledgeable about the double helix of DNA, I knew as much about salmon as I did about half hitches.

Since Idaho had started their hatchery programs they'd had pretty poor returns. They figured the salmon might better imprint where to return to if they hatched in the creeks and spent the entire winter there, rather than being dumped from the hatchery into the creeks every spring. My job was to give them a sporting chance.

In the fall, a small floodgate at the head of the channel was opened wide to get as much flow as possible, making it harder for it to freeze. In the spring the flow had to be nearly cut off since the silt from the runoff was heavy enough to bury the fish hiding in the rocks. They'd have to swim all the way to the Pacific that summer, but they wouldn't yet be strong enough to keep from being buried alive by silt.

Every morning my job was to walk to the channel, a few hundred yards from my tent and, if ice had formed on the end, where there was a small drop off, chop it away. The theory was to let ice and snow build up over the channel, insulating it, while keeping the water beneath from being blocked and freezing solid—along with all those tiny fish.

That first morning I inspected the channel, full of the great responsibility entrusted to me. But my boss had already set the headgate the way he wanted it for the rest of the winter and there wasn't a hint of ice anywhere. I looked at the crystal clear water. There was no trace of my fish, all hidden deep down in the rocks. There was nothing for me to do.

That was my job. That's all. If there was ice it would take fifteen minutes a day, including the walk. The rest of the time was on my hands, but I had to be at that channel every day. For seven more months. Taking care of fish I couldn't see, somehow filling up the other twenty-three and a half hours of each day.

I called it a day and started back to the tent. I took the long way, knowing I could spare the time, inspecting the island the channel formed between itself and the river. I hopped over the headgate but stopped when Boone whined. She was hopping from foot to foot, crouching and standing, not quite able to make the leap. I started back to her, calling her name at the same time and slapping my thigh, and she made the jump, coming up just short. I heard the scrabble of her claws against the concrete wall of the gate, then the splash.

She fell on the creek side, rather than into the slow, shallow water of the channel. By the time I saw her bob up her legs paddled wildly at air and water alike, not unlike the ladder-climbing look of a drowning person. I hopped from rock to rock until I was able to haul her out by the scruff. She looked cat-like with her hair slicked down, and she was already shivering. She burrowed into my chest, too small to really soak me much. I held her there, wrapping my arms around her to give her warmth and again started back to the tent where I dried Boone off and stoked the fire for her. She lay down on a towel next to the stove and was asleep so fast I wondered if she'd wake up.

I didn't want to leave her but I realized I'd go crazy just sitting there. So while she snoozed I began to unpack my stuff. I settled into the tent, deciding where the little spring frame bed would go, where the plywood table would go. I fidgeted restlessly with every choice, knowing it was important to make good decisions but beginning to suspect that the very act of keeping busy might be the most important part of all my tasks.

Down the right side of my tent I set up the old wooden cabinets we'd found at Magruder. My bed and the kindling pile filled up the left, and the table stood between them at the far end, opposite the door. The wood stove sat in the corner, the table to one side, bed to the other. I filled one cabinet with clothes, the other with food. In the short space behind the cabinets I hid the bulky stuff—dog food, beans, and rice. Occasionally I'd glance over to make sure Boone's side was still lifting and falling with her breaths.

When Boone was up and about again we walked out into the meadow. There was really nothing to do there but look at the few sticks of firewood I'd collected with the wardens. I looked in the back of the truck to make sure the chainsaw was still there and I hopped in, Boone scrambling over my lap. The hunt for firewood would eat up a lot of time.

Before they'd left the wardens had cut down one tree, to show me how. To warm up I went to its great fallen hulk and started sawing off branches. Then I began cutting it into chunks that would fit into my stove, about a foot and a half long. Bucking it up, the wardens had said. I was bucking up a tree.

Later, when I cut my first tree down (it was a snag, I'd learned, not a dead tree) I picked one that was leaning so far over it couldn't help but fall that way. I made the wedge cut and then double-checked to make sure it was still leaning the same way. When I began cutting across the rest of the tree I'd cut an inch or two and then glance up, making sure the tree wasn't going to try and pull anything sneaky. Finally I looked up even as I sawed, and at the first indication of a shake I turned the saw off and ran like a rabbit.

When I didn't hear any mighty crash I stopped, keeping another tree between me and my victim. My snag was still standing, swaying more freely than it had before, but still standing. I hid behind the tree, feeling stupid and wondering what to do now, when a beautiful gust of wind sent a great crack through the snag and it began to pitch. When it hit the ground I let out a war whoop I didn't know I had in me. I started to buck her up. Soon I had my shirts off, glad to feel the fall air drying my sweat.

On my third pickup full I found a downed tree that looked good—they all looked pretty good to me, but this one was uphill of the road. I moved the truck into position beneath it and carried my saw up and started bucking. My back hurt from all the bent-over work, and curled shavings clung to my sweating arms, but this was great fun. It kept my mind off everything else.

When I was finished bucking I rolled the first log down the hill and it landed perfectly behind the truck. I grinned, thinking of how long it would have taken me to carry that log all the way down there. The next overshot the road and went a little ways down the hill on the other side. Still it was better than carrying them all, and I didn't stop till one of the logs hit the truck, smashing the taillight and lightly crushing the side of the bed. I ran down the hill to inspect the damage, already sweating the chilly, nervous sweat of embarrassment and fear, so much different from that of work. I couldn't believe what an idiot I was. I stood at the truck swearing, my thrill for firewood cutting instantly gone, wondering how well the wardens knew the truck's collections of dents and dings.

I went to bed that night exhausted, replaying the muffled bounce of that log through the moss and needles right into the side of the truck, hearing the plastic of the light shattering. I swore I'd think before doing anything as stupid as rolling logs right at the truck. The wardens would think I was the world's biggest moron.

5

*T*here were three weeks left in the Idaho elk season when I moved in and there were still elk hunters on the little strip of road surrounded by the Selway-Bitterroot Wilderness Area. In the last days of the season they grew unbearably curious why anyone would keep stacking up more and more firewood, with the season nearly over. When the curiosity finally overwhelmed them, one hunter wandered over to where I worked the splitting wedges and asked what was up.

The story leaked through the hunting camps. Over the next few days, as the camps pulled out, unshaven, woolly, orange-clad men stopped by now and then, offering leftovers from their camps. I collected quite an odd store of staples and nearly empty liquor bottles, mostly different flavors of brandy (apricot, peach, blackberry); stuff that I had never tasted. It was their way of offering condolences, I think. But I could tell they thought I was doing something they didn't have the guts for and I liked to sit in my tent at night and dwell on that.

With all those hunters I was hardly isolated but, knowing so little about anything, I didn't openly seek company. I was pretty hard up for it, but all the hunters looked so much like they knew what they were doing.

And there was the wood gathering. With that to throw myself into I was still able to stave off the long silent winter that lurked ahead. I worked to exhaustion every day and slept as soon as I finished dinner; usually some mix of potatoes and canned ham. One day when the thought of hauling another log was too much to take, I went into the trees behind my tent and started digging a food cache pit, following instructions from one of the Angier books. I dug a hole four feet by four feet by four feet deep and covered it with old planks and dirt, insulating it with hay from the hunt camps. The main thing was to stay so busy there'd be no time for anything else.

So, surrounded by the last people I would see on a regular basis for the next half a year, I did what they did, nodded and waved sometimes, only occasionally being invited over to a camp for a meal and some drinks. I accepted those, but feeling I had nothing to offer, did not reciprocate. And I loved those chilly nights in the warm, smoky tents with the drinks and the lies and the laughing. Boone would sit underfoot, filling out slowly, and I tried not to wonder what it would be like when the only tent on the river was mine.

I made two trips into Missoula before the road closed. There were more of the same send-off parties, even more determined, and I returned to my tent more scared each time.

After my last trip out Rader and several other friends followed me back in the Deerslayer. We spent two days dropping more snags and hauling wood back to my pile, which Rader assured me was approaching ten cords.

We worked like dogs, mainly because that's all I'd done here. But finally they revolted and we went hunting grouse, cooking up a gourmet meal of roasted grouse stuffed with canned corn (one of my staples). We all thought it was delicious and we drank and wrestled like nineteen-year-olds on spring break. I laughed frantically at the smallest jokes, knowing my time was running out, and if they noticed they pretended not to.

It started to snow while they were there, a storm that looked serious this time, though the steep walls of the Selway cut off most of the sky. They decided they'd have to leave a day early, to make sure they'd get over the pass before it snowed shut. I tried talking them out of it, but Rader had made up his mind, and I knew what I was arguing for. When the Deerslayer disappeared I went and sat on the edge of my bed, unable to believe how big and empty that small tent seemed. I hurried outside and walked to the channel, but, as always, there was nothing to be done there, the ice having not yet shown. Instead of going back inside the tent I began to fix the hammer handles they'd shattered at the chopping block. It was busy work and something I'd never done before. I'd already learned not to leave an idle moment, especially in the down times. And if I could pull off something new, the elation over the success could carry me past most of the rough spots, for a little while anyway.

The storm continued in fits and gusts and I had dinner the last two nights of the season with one of the few remaining hunting parties, two brothers, farmers from Idaho. They treated me like a hero for doing what I was doing. I would have given anything to leave with them. If I could have thought of anything, made up any reason that would get me out of there while saving face, I would have lunged at it. But I couldn't. I was in it now.

They invited me to go hunting with them on their last day and I accepted. I planned on hunting for food during the winter, and I wanted to see how it was done. I'd shot some grouse so far, and some of the tiny tree squirrels, but I knew elk or deer would be a different game altogether.

The next morning, as I prepared for the hunt, my boss walked through the flap of my tent. As promised, he was making his last checkup before the pass closed. He said it looked as if I'd settled in well. He kidded me about the stack of firewood I'd amassed, saying how I was set for the winter from hell now, that he at least didn't have to worry about my freezing to death. We walked to the channel and he looked it over and said it looked great, that I'd obviously been doing a fine job. I hadn't done a single thing at the channel yet but look at it every morning, and I wondered what he was seeing.

We walked back to the tent and he pulled a white wooden box

out of the back of his truck. We set it up in the meadow—a weather station I was to keep for the Forest Service. It contained two thermometers, one that stopped at the day's high temperature, the other at the low. I was to record the temperatures each morning and reset the thermometers. A silver precipitation gauge perched atop the box.

When he'd explained the weather station the warden said he'd try to snowmobile in sometime in mid-December, to see how things were going and to bring in my mail. If I found that I needed anything I could hike down to Magruder and call out to West Fork and they'd get the message to him. Then he got in his truck and left. He hadn't been in half an hour.

When he was gone I went over to the brothers' camp and we went hunting, which was really nothing but a slow walk down the trail, looking around. We didn't see anything, though I shot a grouse on the way home, neatly clipping its head with the bullet. They praised the shot and I couldn't believe how good that made me feel. Though the shot was one I was getting used to making, I wanted to take it over and over again, while there was someone there to watch.

The snow kept coming harder as we walked back and when we reached their camp they cased their rifles quickly and began to pack. I went to my camp to get out of their way. From inside my darkened tent I listened to their shouts and the banging of their truck doors, and finally the first roar of their engine.

They pulled past my tent on the way out, leaving their truck idling. They gave me a paper sack full of leftover staples and we shook hands all around. They wished me luck and told me to look them up when I got out, that I was always welcome. I nodded, afraid to talk much, and they climbed into the cab of their truck. I could hear the heater blowing full blast. They waved once more and started off.

When they were gone my meadow was completely empty. After looking around it for a few minutes I hopped in my old truck and started downriver, away from the pass. At the end of the road was Paradise, where there was another summer ranger station, this one so small they called it a guard station. Paradise was also the camp for one of the big outfitters back here. Listening to the awful quiet around my tent I realized I hadn't seen their trucks pull out. I raced through the snow, seeing if I might be in time to talk with them for a while.

When I reached Paradise there were only a few of the guides left and the outfitter. They were loading the last horses and lashing down the last of their tarps. They took quick sips of beer as they worked and when they decided they were ready to roll we all went into the cook tent to have one last drink. There was an old man in the tent, who'd been drinking all along. He was a friend of theirs who'd just driven in for the day.

I'd begun to feel foolish even before they asked what they could do for me, what brought me down to Paradise? I didn't know these people well, and I didn't have any reason I could give them.

I had a quick drink with them, but the old man was badly drunk and it was not comfortable in the tent. When they asked what I thought about staying in here all winter I said it seemed all right. These weren't talkative men, and pretty soon they said they really had to be getting out while the getting was good. They said they'd be back in sometime, in January probably, on snowmobiles, to hunt mountain lion. I'd never heard of that before, but I said, "Good. I'll see you guys then. Stop on by for a drink." I didn't have anything to give them except half shots of weird brandies, but it seemed to be the only social thing to do back here.

While we talked the drunken old man left on his own. I wondered about his driving, but I was in a group of older men, men who knew everything there was to know about this place, men who even knew how to hunt mountain lions—an animal I didn't even know lived here. So, I didn't say anything but, "See you in the winter," before climbing back into my truck and driving away, wishing I'd had the strength to never come. I'm sure they saw through to the frightened kid needing company, and I didn't like that I'd let them do that.

Not a quarter of a mile down the road I saw the old man's truck upside down in the ditch, saplings crushed and broken all around it. I jumped down and found the old man still inside, sobbing hysterically about the other guy, "Oh my God, he's dead. I killed him." I could see a long tear in his blue jeans, revealing nothing but red where I should have been able to see his skin.

Though officially I'd been a lifeguard at Lake Mead, I'd wound up doing all sorts of rescue work, including car wrecks, so I was on familiar ground now. The old man was thrashing around so much I knew his spine wasn't broken, but as I worked on getting him out he kept crying for me to leave him alone. "Leave me here. Get the other guy." He didn't have any teeth and he was hard to understand.

I hadn't known that he'd left with anyone else, but I circled the truck looking for someone pinned underneath, then did a wider pass through the willows. I couldn't find a trace of another person.

Back at the truck I finally, forcefully, fished him through the window. I started to get tough with him, telling him to be quiet, I needed to look at his leg. He was blubbering now, and I couldn't understand anything he said. I laughed though, checking his leg, the one I thought had been covered in blood. The red was the red of his union suit, exactly the same color as the one I wore.

I hauled the old guy to the road and drove him back to camp. The others surrounded my truck and grumbled at the old man. I asked about the other guy he was so worried about and they said there was no one else, that's just the way he got when he drank.

They shoved him in the cab of a truck and said thanks for bringing him back. I asked about the truck in the ditch. They said they'd worry about it in the spring.

With the leftover adrenaline still in my blood I couldn't believe they treated this all as something to expect. No big deal. But I'd been in the ditch, arguing and struggling with a hysterical, delusional old man who could very easily have been killed, a man they'd let get in his truck without a whisper.

For the first time I saw into these people, these hunters I held in such awe. For the first time I understood there were things I knew much more about than they did. If their friend had been hurt I could have done something. They wouldn't have even known. They were, after all, just people.

I said goodbye again and drove back down the snow-covered road to my tent. I stayed outside, splitting a little kindling, so I'd be out when the trucks from Paradise drove past. In less than an hour they rumbled by and though I waved, they didn't stop, or even slow down. They waved back and the guy driving the horse truck honked his horn. I waved again and watched their rigs disappear into the trees at the edge of my clearing, racing the snowstorm that was closing the pass. I stood quietly, my ax dangling from my hand, listening for how long it took the twists of the canyon to silence even the roar of their engines and the banging of their trailers through the rutted road. The sound was gone within a minute and that fast it seemed as if I had been staying in this meadow a lot longer than three weeks. And that canyon seemed a lot narrower and a lot quieter.

The snow covered their tracks before the day was done and soon it was hard to believe I had ever been anything but alone. The snows even took the last of the yellows from the trees and buried them, until it seemed I would have only the sky's faded winter blue and the green-blacks of the unending ridges of spruce and fir and pine.

That evening I walked through the snow to the salmon, the heavy, wet flakes drifting down windlessly, more quietly than would have seemed possible, muffling the world.

Boone had grown enough that she ranged a little ahead as I performed my nightly duties at the channel, which consisted solely of looking dumbly at the black water flowing over fish I couldn't see. Snow collected on her back and on my shoulders. The night began to wrap around me and the next six months grew in my head—ranging out ahead of me forever.

6

I'd realized the snow would close the pass. I'd realized it would
drive the last of the hunters away. I'd even realized it would
close the little bit of road I had for my truck. But, when it kept
falling the day after even the outfitters had pulled out, and
then the day after that, and after that, I began to realize what else the
snow had done. My wood gathering was nearly over.

I bucked up one more tree, but the snow covering the logs
soaked me and hid branches that tripped me while I concentrated on
carrying logs. Sidehilling once, carrying the heavy butt end of a tree,
I stepped on a branch that pointed downhill. My foot whipped out
from under me so fast I fell backward before I quite knew what was
happening. I landed flat on my back and the log pile-drived into my
chest; I lay there, the paralyzing feeling of being unable to draw the
slightest breath swarming through me. I fought to hold back the
panic, remembering how many times I'd had the wind knocked out
of me playing football as a kid. When I finally began to suck air again,
I decided I had enough wood.

Instead of killing time with wood gathering, I began to spend
days splitting all the wood piled beside my tent. When even that was
done I had a mountain of firewood. I leaned against it, knowing if the
snow hadn't forced me to stop I would have kept at it all winter, my
version of a mind-numbing assembly line job.

But I would have had to explain the huge stacks of wood to the wardens, who'd made it clear that wood cutting was a loathsome chore to be gotten over as quickly as possible. I could picture the disbelief in their faces, the way they'd glance at each other and not at me. So maybe I wouldn't have kept on cutting endlessly. Or maybe I would have. I could have built a solitary bonfire every night, getting rid of the evidence. I pictured how the flames and embers would race into the black sky, reflecting off the dark walls of the canyon. I'd stand alone beside the leaping fire, like some sort of Druid calling on the powers of hell, but really I'd be nothing but a bored kid, killing time without wanting anyone catching me at it.

I pushed myself off the stack of wood, ten rows of it as tall as I was, stretching the full length of my tent, sixteen feet. I went inside and did the math. Over eleven cords. I smiled, feeling I'd accomplished something. They'd said at the worst I'd need ten. I'd beaten that.

I walked outside and looked at the wood again, wondering what there was to do now. I strolled around the meadow. I hadn't really thought this out. There was no more wood to cut, and I didn't have anything else to do. Agreeing to come in here, I'd had some sketchy idea of freedom, of having to answer to no one, of being able to do exactly and only what I wanted. Now it seemed that I'd overlooked the simple fact that though I could do anything I wanted, at any time, there really wasn't anything to do. It was a feeling as panicky as having that log crush the air from my lungs. What if claustrophobia pressed in that hard? What if I just went nuts in here for lack of anything to do?

I hurried to my tent and slipped my little rifle over my shoulder. I'd go hunting. Gather food. I started up Indian Creek, faster than I needed to, plowing snow with my shins, concentrating much harder than was necessary. This was serious business. Hunting was a job I needed to do. With the wood gathering finished I had to be able to convince myself of that.

When I didn't find any game I practiced with my rifle. Rader had insisted I bring in a huge amount of ammo, thousands of rounds, and

I began to plink. I shot down pine cones, clipped the ends off dead twigs, bulls-eyed knotholes. When that got slow I walked to the river and threw sticks into the rapids. I'd shoot as fast as I could at the racing, tossing, twisting sticks. At first water would cannonade into the air around the sticks, but as I continued to practice, the sharp crack of the rifle would slap through the canyon and the stick would only jerk with the impact. My rifle held five shots. Soon I was disappointed if I missed with any of them.

When I was growing up in Milwaukee I used to entertain myself endlessly on walks to and from school by throwing things—snowballs in winter, dirtballs or stones in summer. I'd pick trees or street signs as targets and throw as I walked, imagining hits or near misses on everything from battleships to World Series strike zones. I began to think of bullets as nothing but high-tech snowballs.

If I was actually out hunting I took more and more difficult shots, all part of the game I'd developed to make this more serious, more challenging. A miss could ruin my day. Grouse, the big prize, would routinely duck if I missed, then sit and blink and give me another chance. Marksmanship was not nearly as crucial as I pretended.

The first hints of ice appeared in the channel and I began checking it twice a day, scouring away every last scrap of ice—something to do. Walking back from the channel one evening I saw a grouse perched in a tree near my tent. It was still a long way off, maybe seventy-five yards, and that I spotted him at all was a fluke. But the shapes of my prey were becoming distinctive, something that stood out more quickly than other things.

Instead of moving in slowly, from tree to tree, as I should have, I sat down where I was and aimed and fired, just to make it that much harder. The grouse fluttered down, flapping wildly out of control, a clear sign it'd been hit in the head. In college I'd learned that the brain was a vast controller of functions. Rather than being just an initiator of action, it spent a great deal of time inhibiting random action. A chicken runs around after its head has been chopped off for that reason.

I stood up proudly, just stopping before I turned to no one to say, "Wow, did you see that?"

When I reached the bird it was still flopping weakly in the snow, its head completely gone. My pride at hitting something the size of a nickel with open sights at that kind of range diminished a little. I bent down and picked up the bird, feeling its muscles twitching, dying down as the nerve impulses lost the last of the energy needed to operate.

Then I noticed the fresh snow beyond the area marred by the fluttering of the grouse. A fine spray of crimson dusted the snow, no trace bigger than the head of a pin. That, I realized, almost with surprise, was from the sudden explosion of an animal's head. I wasn't shooting at something the size of a nickel. I was shooting at living things. I picked up my rifle carefully; I was not throwing snowballs at street signs.

At night I began to read. I went through my manuals and my Foxfire books again and again, because they were all I had. I took great interest in learning how to split cedar shingles from logs, or how to scald pigs to remove their hair. Because there was nothing else to do, I became an expert on several things I would never do.

I also read all sorts of advice on trapping. I remembered the bag of traps I had, my mountain man stuff. I spent a day boiling the traps to remove the oil that would give off telltale scents, then I boiled them again, mixing in a bag of powder I'd purchased—logwood dye. I didn't know what it was for, but the books said it was necessary. It turned the steel black.

I began to make lists, too. I picked patterns for the moccasins I would make, set up ambitious trap lines on paper. I had things-to-do lists a page long that I would go over at night, convincing myself that tomorrow would be a busy day.

I wrote the lists in the notebooks I'd brought for my journal-writing class, and last thing every night I'd write down what I'd done during the day. There were some pretty short entries. But now and then I'd get going and the power of the words to return me to

Missoula or even Wisconsin kept me at the journal, kept the entries growing longer.

During the day, when I wasn't out carrying my rifle, or chopping at my stacks of wood, most of this early time was spent adjusting to my tent and the woods. Snowshoeing was a snap. In one day the twitching of my groin muscles taught me to lift the shoes over each other, not to waddle with legs spread wide enough for the shoe's width. The short, rounded shoes were much more manageable in the thick timber. But the longer shoes held my weight up higher, and in the open I could nearly fly, powder spraying.

I learned to cook, sort of. I rigged an old grill I found into a rack for my wood stove. By letting the fire burn down to coals and regulating the dampers I was able to bake. The heat regulation took some time to iron out, though, and I made ash out of most of my early projects.

Small failures like that could set off some desperate swings—to loneliness so powerful it could make me fight for breath. Then tiny victories, like pulling my first golden loaf of bread from the wood stove, would send me into idiotic charges through my meadow, laughing and carrying on as if I'd just won the lottery.

Each one of those victories, as minor as they were, cut a piece out of the loneliness that always skulked nearby, in the dark patches of trees, in the black water trying not to freeze over, even in the way the river talked at night, taking on voices it never had in the day. A hollow began to take shape for me in the woods, and I grew comfortable in it.

Thanksgiving came and I planned to let it go without any fanfare. I never was much for holidays. But as the day dragged on I began to imagine what was going on at home. Everyone would be there, everyone except my sister living in Germany, working as a medical technician. And me, living in a tent, working at killing time.

My grandmothers, the ladies, would have been picked up and driven to our home, and the table would be laden with all that food. Everyone would be telling stories, cutting each other off, listening, anxious to get their chance to speak. The thermostat would be twisted up high for the ladies. I sat alone in my tent, wearing my usual union suit and wool pants and two wool shirts, sewing a piece of sheepskin into a mukluk.

Suddenly I knew I had to keep up the tradition, even if just for myself. I threw the mukluk aside and started into the trees, for the first time actually needing to find a grouse, needing to have its golden roasted breast as the centerpiece of my feast.

I went up the south side of Indian Creek, where the trees and brush were thick, giving good cover to ruffed grouse. I hiked a long way without finding anything. During a breather I turned, seeing my tent far below me, snuggled into the juncture of the Selway and Indian Creek, the neatly stacked wood like a fortress wall beside it, a small twist of smoke still curling from the stove pipe. The big river threw off splinters of sun, and as I looked up I saw the clouds racing by low, splitting around the peaks and ridges that closed off the river. I turned to Boone and said, "That's my home, Boone." I couldn't believe how perfect it looked, and I wished there was some way to tell stories about it right now to the gathering in Milwaukee.

It wasn't until the return hike, getting desperate now for a grouse, that I crossed tracks—perfectly formed bird footprints in the soft snow. I glanced up from the trail just in time to see the grouse at the end of his tracks, looking over his shoulder at me, trying to keep a tree between us. I lifted my rifle and had him, but with the brush between us I hesitated and suddenly he flushed, breaking wildly through the branches, arcing downhill, where I caught quick, short flashes of his flight through the trees.

I swore, angry at not having taken the shot when I had the chance, too anxious to have this grouse for dinner tonight. I couldn't believe I'd screwed it up even after having the luck to find one. I searched for nearly an hour, finally getting him sneaking along a branch. Another head shot. I gutted him and plucked him as I walked, but I was already beginning to realize that this poor old bird was not going to take me to Milwaukee tonight.

I prepared the grouse as best I could, adding carrots and onions and potatoes, but I had the stove too hot and the bird came out pretty dry. Cooking on such short notice, I didn't have the time to make any bread, or coffee cake, or rice pudding—newly discovered recipes I'd already begun to savor as the spice of special occasions.

I thought again of my family, and everyone else's, all sitting down to well-planned get-togethers, and I wound up leaving my dry little dinner and walking around in the silent trees until long after it was fully dark. After that it was comforting just to get back to my tent and light the lantern. To be able to see again.

7

To recover from the low I'd made for myself over the holiday I threw myself into trapping. Gathering all my traps, I set them everywhere. I had no idea how to do it, or even many thoughts on what it was I was actually doing. I saw marten sign all over, and set traps for them. I learned fairly quickly that the marten tracks were really squirrel tracks. In the next few days I caught a squirrel in one of those traps and it was frozen solid by the time I found it. I didn't feel very good about that, and I pulled the rest of the marten sets. I told myself that I'd reset them once I knew where the marten were, but if I'd been forced to, I would have admitted that I couldn't really justify killing something that way—not just for money.

In another set I caught a snowshoe hare and it wasn't frozen solid. It was very much alive, bleating in terror at my approach. I never knew rabbits could make any sound, let alone one as chilling as that.

I killed the hare as quickly as I could, and I ate it that night. It was delicious, a welcome change from my diet of rice or potatoes with the occasional squirrels or grouse thrown in, but it was getting hard to keep up the excitement for any of the trapping.

I still left most of my traps out though, unable to face the loss of another major occupier of time. I left out all the coyote traps. They didn't hurt anything. Coyotes are smart and I never came close to catching one. Now and then I'd see their tracks approach my bait, wander cautiously around and then leave. I hadn't done everything right about smell.

I also left the traps around the channel. I could tell by tracks that something was getting into the channel at night, eating my salmon. My boss, the warden, had told me to have at whatever messed with the fish, even to the point of blasting the ouzels that would walk the bottom of the channel, picking off whatever they could. I liked watching the little slate-gray birds bobbing nervously at the stream edges, their eyes flashing white as they blinked with every dip. Occasionally I'd see them walking along the bottom, strolling as casually as if they had not yet realized they were under water.

I never looked at one through rifle sights.

But unseen things that moved at night were different from screaming hares or small dipping birds. I could not watch the night animals, could never even see them. Without the snow giving them away, I would not have even known they were there. Curiosity played no small part in my willingness to set traps for them. And once the traps were out, every morning held an anticipation it hadn't had before, a wondering what would be out there, what would I find, not unlike what Christmas morning had been as a kid. Maybe something would be in one of the traps, maybe today I'd find what else lurked out here, what shared the river with me.

On the first day of December I went, like every other morning, to chop the ice out of the channel and check the traps. After clearing the ice I leaped the headgate, Boone now clearing it easily behind me, and I began to check the traps on the island, which appeared to be a thoroughfare for most of the tracks that led to the channel.

The first trap was empty, same as always, but when I turned the corner at the next set, there was a raccoon straining at the end of the trap chain, his right rear foot in the trap. He lay down when he saw me, the chain stretched taut in the opposite direction. A circle, the radius of the chain length, was cleared through the snow around the trap anchor, down to bare earth.

The raccoon did not bleat like the hare had. It did not give up either. Through the long hair I could see every muscle tight, steadily straining in one last try to pull free. When I moved he glanced back at me, as if wondering what was going to happen now, his eyes bright in the dull black stripe masking his face.

I was wondering the same thing. I saw again the churned up ring of dirt and needles, saw what it told about the raccoon's last hours, and I wanted to end everything as quickly as I could. Passages from my how-to books flashed through my mind, advice from hardened old trappers about pelt value and preparation and animal habits. Fur-bearers were only shot as a last resort. Clubbing was messy. The preferred method of dispatch, when possible, was stepping on the animal's torso, pushing from back to front, folding the rib cage, crushing the lungs and heart between the sternum and spine. CPR worked on the same principle, only differing in degree of force. I'd read that paragraph twice, fascinated by the simple mechanics of it, the ease with which something so brutally effective could be spelled out.

But, with this raccoon pulling at the chain and staring at me, my thoughts had nothing of this kind of cool order. I jumped forward, my heavy boot pinning the raccoon to the circle of earth he'd cleared, and I shifted my weight. Even through the rubber sole and felt liner of my boot I could feel the ribs collapse, accordion-like, following the downward lean of all mammal ribs. The raccoon's eyes bulged slightly, in surprise perhaps. I turned my face away, studying the fork in a twisted little cottonwood. Though there was no struggle beneath my foot I stood there a long time. Each morning, when I wondered what I would find in the traps, I'd managed not to actually picture what a success would mean.

When I stepped off of the raccoon I watched for a trace of movement, some slight sign of struggle for breath, but there was nothing like that, nothing at all. As Boone moved in for a sniff I noticed the raccoon's toes, only held in the trap by the last knuckle or so. He'd almost gotten away.

I stepped on the trap's spring, opening the jaws and releasing the foot. I took off my mitten and felt the bones. None were broken. I sat in the cleared circle and pulled the raccoon into my lap, surprised by how heavy he was. I petted his fur smooth, erasing the mark of my boot.

This was my first real success trapping. I'd caught a furbearer. I was trying to be a mountain man but instead I touched the circle of frozen dirt in the snow and pictured the raccoon running around and around and around.

He had been decimating the fish, I reminded myself. But I still had not seen one of those salmon and, for crying out loud, there were two and a half million of them. They were meant to take losses. And I could see this raccoon, and I could touch him and I could picture what had happened to him. His hands were shaped a lot like mine.

I pulled most of my traps after that.

I spent the rest of that day carefully skinning the raccoon and pouring over my *Foxfire* books, comparing recipes for raccoon and studying the techniques for tanning the skin. For the next few days I worked on the hide, scraping away fat and flesh, soaking it in an alum solution. I'd decided I was going to make a coonskin cap.

But the skin had to soak for days, and that wouldn't occupy me much. I walked outside and sat on a stump, scratching at Boone's ears, again wondering what I would do all winter. It hadn't been snowing much recently and I began to wonder if I could still drive to Magruder, the summer ranger station.

Eventually I crawled into the cab of the truck. The wardens had said I should pull the battery when the snow grounded it for the winter. The snow was pretty close to that deep, but suddenly I wanted to chance a final trip. I hadn't driven for quite a while, and I decided to let the truck make the decision for me. I pumped the gas and turned the key. The engine fired and caught hold and began to idle. I was on my way to Magruder.

The old ranger station, which had walls of wood, not canvas, also had a propane stove, and a propane water heater, and a bathtub. With the stove's slow steady heat I could make a huge batch of baked beans, something I couldn't do with my wood stove, which was made for heating, not cooking. Baked beans was the only recipe I had for beans, though I had a fifty-pound sack of them.

As the truck warmed up I scurried through my tent, packing beans, onions, and everything else I thought I might need, excited again to have a project.

When I started the drive everything seemed all right. Sometimes, looking in the mirror, I could see that the muffler or something like that was cutting its own rut in snow, but I drove slowly, knowing I had all the time in the world, and that I didn't need to worry about meeting anyone coming the other way.

Somehow the snow got deeper the farther I went. Five or six miles away from my tent I was plowing snow with the front bumper and, even chugging along in first gear, the truck would occasionally begin to decide its own course, the tires riding a drift instead of crushing through to road. I'd let off the gas then, once forgetting to depress the clutch, stalling the truck in nothing flat. I sat behind the wheel, breathing hard, covered instantly in sticky, stupid sweat, wondering what the wardens would think when they snowmobiled past the dead, half-buried truck on their first mail run.

I would have turned around if I could have seen the edge of the road. But the snow pillowed everything, blurring what were once sharp lines, and though I could imagine the wardens squeezing to one side of the road to snowmobile past the buried truck, I didn't want to picture them standing at the side of the road, off their snowmobiles, staring down into the river at their old green pickup, the black water of the Selway lapping all around it.

So I plowed on, never exceeding five, or at the most ten, miles an hour, the whole time wishing I'd never left, hoping the snow would hold off so I could get back with the truck, while at the same time wishing it would snow monumentally, burying deeply my foolish tracks. Boone sat quietly, tall enough now to look out the window at the snow and the river.

When I finally reached Magruder I remembered the hill. I knew I'd never make it up that, so I stopped the truck above the ranger station and slid down the slope, glad to feel my feet under me again. I unlocked the door and opened the water lines, a procedure the wardens had gone over with me. I stoked the wood furnace and started making a quadruple batch of baked beans. Once the propane had heated the water tank I started my bath, getting into the cold iron tub and running the water around me, so I could get used to it as it filled, keeping the water as hot as I could stand.

Then I lay back, eyes closed. It was my first bath in weeks, and the last one I could imagine having for months.

I relaxed as much as possible, but I couldn't shut out the return ride. I'd half planned on spending the night, but now I crawled out of the tub and drained all the water lines, let the fire die out in the furnace, and when the beans were done I shut off the propane and shuffled back through the snow to the truck. I couldn't risk a night storm closing the road for good. I had to get out of here.

The pot of beans snuggled into the snow filling the bed of the truck and Boone hopped into the cab, spraying snow everywhere. I started up the engine and lurched out, not knowing when I'd see Magruder again.

The ride home was easier, letting the truck follow its own ruts. Before I reached the tent it began to snow again, big, heavy flakes, and I was glad I'd returned when I could. Back at Indian Creek I pulled the battery from the truck and stuck it into the corner of my tent. I was on foot from now on.

Sitting in my gloomy tent that night, I couldn't put my trip out of my mind. I'd pulled it off, but I knew it had been a mistake, an enormous risk to take for a pot of baked beans and a bath. If I'd had a moment of bad luck the truck would have sat all winter, like the old man's at Paradise, a solid reminder of a moment of fear, of a day I'd inched close to the panic of having nothing to do, inched so close I'd driven my truck into the Selway for a pot of beans.

But at the same time I realized the advantage of isolation. No one would ever know about it. The snow was an ally now, burying every sign of whatever I might do. I could understand and forgive my own foolish decisions. It was the fear of having other people scrutinize my actions that I could not bear—people who only visited this place and could not understand what it was like to stay here.

I turned out the lantern and climbed into my flimsy bed in the dark, the layers of blankets and sleeping bags a reassuring weight over me. I thought of isolation, but I drifted off simply listening to the voices of the river moving along its rocky path, sometimes almost discerning words, or long stretches of distant classical music, like I'd heard as a kid in bed, the symphonies my father listened to coming straight through the walls.

It did not snow much that night, not as much as I would've guessed, not nearly enough to cover my tracks, and the next morning the outfitter from Paradise and one of his guides, Brian, pulled up to my tent on their snowmobiles. They were the first snowmobiles I'd ever seen in action, and I was stunned by their loudness.

They shut off their machines—I would quickly learn they were not called mobiles, but machines—and the outfitter, a crusty, taciturn man in his fifties, asked if I'd just driven to Magruder. The tracks led right to my truck, and I wondered who else he might think would be driving around back here. I laughed a little, feeling the blood coming into my cheeks, and I said, "Yes."

"Musta been a ride," he said.

I agreed and he asked, "You about done driving?"

I said I was and he said, "Good. Your tracks screw up the road. Hard to keep the machines from sliding into them."

My blood was full into my cheeks by then. They said something about pulling out some stuff from Paradise that they'd forgotten before, but I barely heard them. I'd never guessed I'd messed up the road. They roared off then, saying again that they'd be back in January for the lion season.

For the first time since I'd moved in I regretted that my isolation wasn't complete. Maybe I was always going to have to look over my shoulder, never sure of who might pop over the pass, who might catch me doing something stupid, something only a greenhorn would pull.

On their way out they stopped for another second. The outfitter wanted to buy a six-point elk rack I'd found and carried back to my tent. The antlers were still attached to the skull and he said he could use it. I didn't know what for; I'd just thought it was neat. He said he'd give me fifty bucks for it and I said fine, hoping it would atone for the damage I'd done to the road.

The two of them stood quiet as ever, while the outfitter pulled out his checkbook. He said something about not having expected to need any money this trip. He passed the checkbook to his guide and had him write out the check for him, then the outfitter signed it.

They were back on their snow machines, roaring away, the elk skull lashed to their trailer, before I realized that the outfitter didn't know how to write.

8

Once the outfitters were gone, not to return until January, I knew I had some time to myself. The wardens were scheduled to appear with my mail in ten days, on the thirteenth. During those ten days I continued to hunt, but the trapping was already over. That big time-killer had lasted nearly two weeks.

And hunting had already become little more than carrying a rifle while I walked in the hills, filling out the days. I still knocked off the occasional grouse—ruffeds down low, blues up high—and snowshoe hares now and then, but my staple continued to be the little red tree squirrels. I needed three, at the very least two, to make any sort of meal, and it was slow eating, picking through the little bones, but they really were pretty good. Like eating a chicken about an eighth normal size. Small bones. I had plenty of time to pick through them.

As the snow got deeper, however, the squirrels began to burrow through it, going from their dens to their caches of pine cones, never exposing themselves to the bitter cold of the air, or to quick eyes of hawks or coyotes or martens or me. And, though I had two years of a wildlife biology degree under my belt, I'd mismanaged my grouse population. I had to walk farther and farther to have a hope of finding one of them.

Most importantly, I was a mountain man, not a squirrel eater. I began to leave my little .22 behind, lugging around my mountain man rifle instead, the muzzle-loading .54 caliber Hawken. I became, by idea alone, a big-game hunter, and I suffered a spectacular lack of success. I would find tracks, and even once broke something out of the thick cover at the edge of the river, but never saw it.

Yet, the same snow that drove the squirrels under also drove the game out of the mountains the hunters had pushed them into. I opened my tent flap one morning to a herd of about sixty elk, blowing steaming breath into the air above the meadow. They saw me first and all that day, carrying my heavy mountain man rifle, I learned about the disappearing qualities of large game. Another embarrassment.

So I carried the heavy rifle and ate oatmeal breakfasts, bread lunches, and rice dinners. Every meal was a reminder of my lack of skill, and though the warden's visit was getting close, and I should have been growing concerned about hiding my hunting (our tacit agreement), I continued to hunt, as if killing and caring for four or five hundred pounds of elk meat would be nothing more complicated than picking up a grouse and carrying it home.

Seeing the elk in my meadow threw me into a big-game hunting fever. The fact that I found tracks there every morning, proof that the elk spent the night not eighty yards away, practically rubbing my nose in it, did not do anything to make me think more clearly.

One night, with the warden's visit only three days away, I sat in my tent absorbed in my usual nighttime activities of drinking tea and rereading the *Foxfire* book, attempting to understand the arcane habits of Ozark people, and trying to get something on my battery AM radio. It was a clear night though, with no clouds to deflect radio waves into my canyon. On heavy, snowy nights I could pick up several western Idaho stations and two of the high-powered California stations, one in L.A., another in San Francisco. But that night, nothing but static.

Finally, full of tea, I went outside to pee before going to bed. I ducked through the tent flap and stepped into a bright silver world. The full moon had risen above the wall of mountains hemming me in and now shone down upon my snow-whitened world. The flat fields of undisturbed snow reflected the light back up and the trees threw it every which way, until finally there were barely any shadows. I stood in awe, only slowly following my foot trails through the snow into my meadow, unable to believe the ghostly light.

I was nearly laughing, so incredible were my surroundings, and I whispered, "Check this out, Boone." Then my meadow erupted.

There were a few quick, odd, rasping barks, but mainly all I heard was movement, the heavy sounds of big animals breaking quickly away, breathing hard, throwing snow, crushing through the thick timber. I crouched in time to see the fleeting shapes of elk vanishing into the dark line of trees across the meadow and, even surrounded by the quicksilver light, I swore. I'd stumbled into the middle of a herd, the whole time gawking up at the ridges, picking out details I'd never guessed I'd see beyond the bright of day. And now, once again, the game was gone.

I held up my finger though, at arm's length, and studied my nail. I could make it out perfectly. I wondered about the brown sights of my rifle. I moved quickly to my tent and came back out with the Hawken. In the center of the meadow I could line up the sights easily. Back in the trees it was more doubtful. If I was standing in a ray of moonlight it would work. I aimed at black tree trunks, approximating the dark sides of elk, and thought it was possible.

I followed the path of the elk into the timber. The temperature was a little below zero and the snow was light powder. It muffled every trace of sound, even the shuffling of my snowshoes. I stalked silently, slipping from one patch of trees to the next, holding my breath to kill even that sound. But, eventually, the tingling anticipation drained away. I no longer believed elk lurked around every tree trunk. And in the thick stuff it really was too dark to sight a rifle. I began to stay in the open, though I doubted the elk were doing the same. Finally I was carrying my rifle over my shoulder, gawking again, at the way the moon transformed a lone spruce into a towering cone of pewter shine.

I walked until one that morning, hunting for maybe the first thirty minutes. The rest of the time I was simply watching. The moon edged down over the other side of the river's cut before I returned to my darkened tent and slipped between the heavy covers.

I got up late the next morning, not having stayed up past ten in months. I was still rubbing sleep from my eyes when I stepped out of my tent, once again scattering my resident elk herd. I spent the rest of the day chasing them, futilely. But I came up with a plan.

That night, as the moon was coming up, I double-checked the meadow for elk. They weren't there yet, and I edged up the horse ramp near my tent. Used for moving horses in and out of trailers, the ramp was the only high point around. From its top I could spy on the entire clearing. I swept a body-wide strip clear of snow and returned to the tent for my blankets and rifle. I made a little bed on the ramp, drawing a white sheet over the top of everything for camouflage. Then I poked my rifle over the lip of the ramp and waited.

By this time I'd completely overlooked what shooting an elk in front of my tent would do. I never stopped to picture what the meadow would look like after that. The wardens were coming in two days but I only thought about finally eating steaks, steaks I had procured through my own cunning and wit and firepower.

It was cold out—six below—but I waited, shivering. The moon cleared the ridge and the meadow's every detail leapt into focus. I tested my sights and swung them around the meadow. I covered everything from here. Nothing could get away. I waited. And waited.

When I woke up the moon had set over the other ridge. It was dark out, black. I could feel falling snow touching me, melting against my cheek. I sat up stiffly, hunching into myself, startled by how cold I was. No stars shone. The Selway was socked in. Fumbling blindly for my tent, I walked into a guy line and followed it inside.

I got my stove going full blast and lugged my blankets in. My body heat had melted most of the snow that had tried to bury me. The rest clung icily to the blankets. I stretched them out on the floor to dry and growled at Boone when she curled up on them. I took off my wet clothes, put on dry ones and just before going to bed I stuck the rifle barrel out the door and pulled the trigger. The hammer fell and the percussion cap popped, a sickeningly small sound compared to the proper booming roar of the rifle. As I'd suspected, the rifle wouldn't fire. Condensation had soaked the powder.

After turning the lantern out I crawled into a couple of the least damp sleeping bags, listening to the ticks and poppings of the stove. What a fiasco. Sleeping through a snowstorm on a horse ramp twenty yards from my bed. Soaking myself and my rifle. The elk could have trampled me if they'd felt like it. I closed my eyes and rolled over, wondering how sick of rice I'd get after eating it for half a year.

The next morning it finally began to dawn on me that the wardens were due in. I stayed inside all day, the fire roaring away, drying blankets. When we'd pitched the tent one of the wardens had found an old roll of indoor/outdoor carpet at Magruder, the quarter-inch-thick stuff. It covered the floor now, holding dirt and wood pile splinters with incredible tenacity. I swept and swept, finally picking the last of the splinters out one at a time.

I hid the raccoon skin, which was tanned now, though somehow, with all my elk hunting, I hadn't found the time to turn it into a hat. I also put all my grouse tails and rabbit feet, my hunting trophies, into a can and buried it in the food cache.

With those preparations out of the way I worked on finishing the letters the wardens would take out. Along with fiddling with the radio and reading the Foxfire books, I spent some time most nights writing letters to friends and family—long letters, ten-, fifteen-pagers. Now that they were actually going to be mailed, I tried to wrap them up. I didn't mention my night on the horse ramp in any of them.

There were also only twelve more shopping days before Christmas. My Thanksgiving debacle was still clear in my mind and in an attempt to avoid that, I'd been working on presents for all my parents and siblings. I packaged my most beautifully dried grouse tails, and a lucky rabbit's foot, and a squirrel skin rug, complete with claws, a joke on a bear skin. For my brothers I sent grouse feet that

I'd dried with the two outside toes curled up, leaving the center toe rigidly extended—a bird foot flipping the bird. I didn't have much to work with.

But, as thin a package as it all added up to, I knew that come Christmas night I'd be able to imagine them opening it, doling out the presents to the proper people. They'd be holding proof that I had not forgotten them, and I would know, that much more surely, that I myself was not forgotten.

I closed the box tightly, wrapping and rewrapping its seams with tape, keeping away the prying eyes of any warden curious about this box of contraband. I wrote "Do Not Open Until Christmas" on the side and set it in the corner. As I finished the letters I stacked the envelopes on top of the box.

But the wardens didn't show. The following day I stayed home, cooking bread, always an all-day project. I was just pulling the loaves from the oven when I heard the distant rumble of snowmobiles. The sound would disappear in different twists of the river canyon, then reappear, always a little closer, a little louder. I stood outside my tent and waited, remembering to call them machines, not mobiles.

My boss and the district wildlife biologist rumbled into the meadow and shot directly for me, pulling up in a spray of snow, grinning. The warden bounced up and shook my hand. He walked into my tent as if he owned it, commenting on the bread, again saying how it looked like I was fitting in just fine. The biologist was new and just followed in the warden's wake.

We walked to the channel together and I told him it'd been dropping to ten below at night for the last few nights, only reaching fifteen in the day. On its own the channel had frozen over and was blanketed with snow. The warden was impressed by the flow of water underneath. He said things looked good and we walked back to the tent.

We stood beside their machines and I asked how the trip in had been. They said it was cold and the biologist pulled a couple of boxes out of his machine and set them on my bed. I noticed the return addresses from Wisconsin. The biologist asked me what I did out here all day, every day. I shrugged and said, "Not much. Mooch around mostly. Write letters." I handed him the letters I'd written and the box I'd packed.

The warden came into the tent then, handing me a sheaf of letters, rubber banded together. I tossed them on the bed to keep from opening them immediately and we talked a minute or two about the game I'd been seeing. "Elk all over the place," I said.

The biologist said he thought his wife would think it'd be neat to stay in here for a few days. He asked if I'd mind getting out for a long weekend, while they took over.

It sounded like a gift from heaven, and I tried not to seem too eager, or desperate when I said that'd be great. He said he'd talk it over with her and get back to me the next time they came in. My boss said that'd be around mid-January, if everything went well.

They worked their way steadily back to their machines as we talked and then they climbed on, shouting, "See you next month," and roared off. They'd been here for about half an hour and I wondered why my boss bothered being a game warden when he always seemed in such a hurry to leave the mountains.

Though they were the first people I'd seen in a couple of weeks, I really wasn't sorry to see them go. The whole time we talked I could barely keep from ripping into the packages and letters sitting on my bed. As soon as the wardens wound out of sight on their noisy machines I was at my mail.

There was something from everyone in my family and most of my friends. I wondered in what order I should read them. My hands trembled a little as I held up the first pages. It was like a party in that tent. I laughed over some of those letters until I had tears in my eyes. Others made me realize how easy this was with all the support I had out there. My parents and my oldest sister, Ellen, sent in books, saying they couldn't imagine living as I was without reading endlessly. I picked up each book like a small treasure and read the covers. There were novels and biographies and short stories. My dad sent all the Sherlock Holmes stories and the Jungle Books, things he remem-

bered my liking as a kid, when he used to read to us. I doubted I'd
ever again bother reading about pig scalding in the Ozarks.

At the bottom of the box, under the books, Ellen even had sent
cake mixes. I laughed at that, wondering how much of an idea they had
about where I really was. But the ones I didn't burn tasted great.

Finally my tent couldn't hold me. I ran out and raced around by
the river, kicking snow into the air. I only stopped long enough to
light the pipe my friends at school had sent, because all mountain men
had pipes. I had never smoked before, and it was fun, although I
couldn't keep it lit. I kept laughing now and then, blowing puffs of
smoke into the darkling blue of the evening. I ran home to reread
everything all over again. I was wearing the pair of sheepskin mukluks
I'd made and my feet felt as light as the snow. I had ice in my beard
and I picked at it as I started all over at the very beginning of the mail.

That night, however, with the mail so read it was dying, the
thrill collapsed and I realized how I missed all those people. It was
a melancholy evening. But already, in the two months I had been in
here, it had softened from the early, desperate loneliness that closed
my throat, to an easy kind I could almost savor.

It was cloudy that night, and I was able to pick up a few of the
Idaho radio stations. I caught most of a Groucho Marx broadcast on
Nostalgia Radio. I laughed all over again, and by the time the station
faded into static I was ready for another sleep.

In the morning I tried to reread my mail again, but it was point-
less—I still remembered every word of every letter and nothing had
changed. I sat down to start writing responses, but it seemed an
awfully crippled way to carry on a conversation. I quit before I'd
really gotten started and I took my rifle and went for a walk. Not just
a walk, I told myself, a hunt.

But I didn't see a thing, could hardly concentrate long enough
to look, and by late afternoon I was back at my tent, back at my mail,
though by now the too familiar words had begun to lose their mean-
ings. Even so, it was all I had.

9

The letter I reread more than any other in that first batch of mail was the one from my father. He and my twin brother, Paul, were in training, he said. They had ordered maps and picked up the last bits of equipment they figured they would need. The day after the Christmas festivities in Milwaukee, they planned to drive out to Darby. From there they would ski up over Nez Perce Pass, following the road, then ski down to the Selway and down the Selway to me. Forty miles. They hoped to make it in two days. Maybe three, but they hoped two, since, after the climb to the summit, it would all be downhill.

Each time I finished that letter I'd look up and see my dark little tent. The tent could be spruced up, but more than the tent I thought of the menu I'd have to offer them, two people who'd skied forty miles just to see me. Oatmeal, bread, rice. If I really got carried away, maybe I'd gourmet the rice by adding a can of peas.

I pictured them skiing through herds of big game, startling deer and elk at every turn. And here I sat with oatmeal, bread, rice. I'd load up my Hawken then and start out, resolved this time not to return until I had something to hang on the meat pole, something with which to stuff my father and my brother. Wild game, something they'd never tasted, something I'd killed alone, because I had to. Me, the hardy survivor, the mountain man.

Along with the letter my dad had sent in books, including the one I was reading now, about Scott's epic trip to the South Pole. I had all sorts of romantic ideas about that kind of stubborn survival, my head still able to ignore the fact that they had all died in the end. I liked to picture Paul and Dad skiing on and on, with myself in the heroic role of providing succor at the end of their trail. The kind of thing that would have saved Scott and his men, if only I'd been there.

But a week of arduous hunting passed and I had yet to point my rifle at anything. With every hour of every day at my disposal I developed the attention span of a five-year-old. Soon I was back to strolling in the evenings, using the last of the day's light, puffing away on my pipe—which I had learned to keep lit—my rifle over my shoulder, held uselessly by the barrel as often as not.

By the time of the winter solstice, the shortest day of the year, I was getting about four hours of direct sunlight, the sun slipping between the Selway's walls between 10:00 A.M. and 2:00 P.M. The rest of the day was indirect lighting, unless I went up high on the ridges. I was eager to have the days begin their lengthening toward the distant spring and I took the day off, lying around and reading, putting logs on the fire, celebrating the low point. From now on every day would be longer, brighter, closer to the end.

So that evening I walked upriver along the beaten path, blowing my first successful smoke rings into the dusk, saying goodbye to the shortest day of all. I'd brought my rifle simply out of habit and I was holding it over my shoulder, by the barrel, when below me on the river something crashed through the willow and rose and snowberry. I looked in time to see a huge, black animal throw itself into one of the last open stretches of the Selway and charge across, coming out on ridiculous, stilt-like legs, swinging a long, bulbous nose in my direction before crashing up the opposite bluff into the trees.

I had my rifle turned around and ready by the time it was gone. I had figured elk, because that's all I had seen. The word *moose* was just working its way forward in my mind when I saw it sidehilling along the opposite bluff—an animal finally larger than a grouse and actually in range. Lining up my sights as I had at targets hundreds of times before, I fired.

In my head I wasn't yet shooting at anything alive. It was a target, and when it broke back into a run after the shot I reloaded frantically, spilling black powder out of the buffalo powder horn I'd made. I ran on my side of the river, paralleling the moose's path until I saw it again. I dropped down and fired. I may as well have been shooting into the sky for all the effect the shots seemed to have.

I was up and spilling more gun powder and ramming another round lead ball down the barrel and the moose was running again. Then it stopped and looked at me and lay down, its head raised normally, looking at me. It didn't seem worried enough about the whole affair.

It was full dusk by this time, nearly dark, and I had to align the sights on the snow and then lower them to the black rectangle of the bedded down moose. I fired a third time, and the moose got up and trotted into another group of trees.

It was too dark to really fire anymore and my target was gone. I looked down the bluff at the green ice of the river, finally starting to think. I wondered how I was going to cross the river, how I was going to look for a moose in the dark.

I ran back to my tent, getting snowshoes and rope and locking Boone into the truck, which had been buried by snow the week before. If I'd wounded the moose I didn't want Boone trotting up to it. I'd become a pretty good shot with the rifle, but I didn't even know if I'd hit the huge animal. When I shot at squirrels or grouse they died instantly and absolutely or they escaped rapidly. This thing hadn't seemed to do either.

Back at the river I slid down the bank and studied the soggy-looking green ice. No place looked any better than another and I held my breath as I began to snowshoe across. The greenish layer of slush oozed through the webbing of my shoes and stuck on top of the cold rawhide. I pictured myself breaking through, my wool clothes soaking up pounds and pounds of water, the cold stinging the breath out of me, being swept downstream beneath the ice. I couldn't believe

I wasn't falling through and I tried unsuccessfully to come up with a plan of action if I did plunge suddenly into the river.

The ice held and I crept up the opposite bank, thinking I was downstream of where I had last seen the moose and that I would cross its track soon. And I did. It was in the heavy timber and I turned on the headlamp I'd barely remembered to grab. Snow started to fall; fat, heavy flakes flashing white as they darted through the light's beam.

The tracks were enormous in the knee-deep snow. There was nothing odd about them, nothing to indicate that a gun had been fired, and fired again, and again. I crept on, not noiselessly on my snowshoes, but close, with the falling snow muffling everything.

Then, caught in the flashlight's beam, a long crimson streak stained the snow—two, actually—one on each side of the moose's track, three or four inches wide, two feet long. I swallowed and put the rifle on half cock, that much closer to firing again. I wondered how stupid it really was to be out in the dark with a wounded moose.

The footprints went on as if the blood wasn't streaked along every few feet. I came across a bed, a flattened spot six feet long, the bottom slushy, brilliant red, more blood than I'd ever seen. The new snowflakes melted when they touched the red. My flashlight swept through the trees around me, lighting only trunks, showing more clearly the complete blackness beyond.

With little idea of what else to do, I continued to follow the tracks, poking the rifle barrel in front of me, really wondering now where the moose was. I was looking up, not wanting to be surprised by the moose's charge, and when I glanced back down I was surprised instead by the end of the tracks. Downhill from the last footprints a long drag mark started. I followed it with the light and at the end, ten yards or so down the hill, was stretched the moose, brought up short against the large, red trunk of a ponderosa pine.

I stood still a moment, watching. The body was much larger than I'd guessed, than I could have imagined. I closed in some, then hesitated. Finally I squatted down, wondering what to do.

Standing up again, ready to run, I lobbed a snowball at it. It thunked solidly into the ribs, drawing no reaction. I moved a little closer, rounding toward its head. I threw another snowball, harder this time. I had never seen anything this big dead. I wondered if it really was dead. I broke off a willow branch and shuffled closer. In one of my old books I'd read that if something didn't blink when touched in the eye it was dead. I tried, reaching the willow stick as far as I could away from my body. It touched the large, round, open, black eye and the eye did not blink. I let out my breath and took a step closer, poking the moose in the eye again.

I moved through the snow the rest of the way and touched the side of the huge body, with my hand. Nothing moved and I knew I had killed it. I sat down on the moose.

I thought of cleaning a snowshoe hare: the precise layout of neatly coiled intestines, the chunkier blocks of stomach and liver, then, sealed off in their own compartment, the bellows of the lungs pillowing the tiny jewel of a heart. A hare was the biggest thing I had ever cleaned and I couldn't imagine that same layout magnified a hundred times or more.

I got off the moose and looked at it once more before trying to roll it onto its back. But it was pinned against the tree and it wouldn't roll. I grabbed one hind leg and pushed and pulled and sweated and swore. Finally I took a rope and tied the leg off to another tree. I was glad no one was with me to see this.

With the leg tied tightly to the tree, I took a deep breath and squatted between the animal's legs. I began to hem and haw with my knife, slicing off globs of hair before I grew impatient and finally cut through the belly. As the hole grew the insides bulged out, blocking my path, getting in the way. I'd read and reread about this: warnings not to cut the guts, not to spill the juices on the insides, not to spoil the meat, and I cut as carefully as I could, and made a mess.

Before I was done I'd stripped off my jacket and shirts down to my union suit. My hair stuck to my head with sweat. I was blood up to my elbows and the snow kept falling, thicker than ever. No wonder they call this butchery, I thought.

Finally the insides lay in a pile outside the empty carcass. I separated the heart and liver. The liver was the size of a six-inch-thick cafeteria tray, the heart as big as my head.

I skinned the moose then, holding my breath with each tentative stroke of the knife, sure I was going to cut a hole, ruining the huge, warm robe I could already feel myself sleeping toastily under. As I skinned I found the path of two of the balls I'd fired, through the ribs behind the shoulder. One had clipped the aorta, only an inch or two above the heart. I found the flattened ball under the skin on the opposite shoulder and put it in my pocket. When I slid the skin out from under the moose and hefted it onto my shoulder I couldn't believe the weight of the wet, black-haired hide. I was exhausted.

I wrapped the hide around my neck, like an enormous towel, and I pinched the heart and liver against my chest with one arm and carried my rifle with the other, and with my headlamp fading I struggled back to the river. By the time I reached it I'd thought of coyotes. What a feast they'd have. I trudged back up to the carcass and peed around it, wondering if that could possibly do any good.

Thinking of the thin green ice, I ferried the pieces over in two trips, growing more frightened each time. On my side of the river I staggered back to my tent. Boone bounded out of the truck, after her first imprisoning since she was a tiny pup. She sniffed suspiciously at the hide and steered clear of it.

I gave her some of the enormous liver for dinner but, with a thousand-pound supply of fresh meat, I was too tired to eat.

The next day, after chopping the thickening ice out of the channel's end, I shuffled back to the kill. The snow had been falling steadily, slowly, and my pee holes were covered. But the moose itself stood out clean, starkly red and white, still warm enough to keep snow from piling on it.

Following the directions I'd read one more time over morning coffee, I cut the moose into quarters, using an ax and a carpenter's saw. I staggered with the quarters to the river, only able to carry the unwieldy weights fifty or sixty feet at a time. Not daring to be on the ice at the same time as the meat, I crossed the river first, then, safely on shore, dragged each piece across with a rope. The technique meant eight crossings of the groaning ice, holding my breath each time.

Once across I found I couldn't carry the pieces and negotiate the steep, snow covered bank at the same time so I tugged them up at the end of the rope. The last quarter hung up in a nest of willows, and instead of sliding back down the bank long enough to clear it, as I should have, I swore and grabbed an extra loop and tugged and yanked like a madman. The quarter bulled through the brush and something gave in my hand, the rope squeezing like a vise around my mittens. In the fifteen-degree air, sweat dripped into my eyes and off my nose and I shouted every swear word I knew, slashing at the rope with my other hand, the rope taut enough to sing.

Not until I had all the pieces on top of the bank on my side of the river did I realize I had to think about this, that brute strength wasn't going to be the answer. I took an hour off to build a sled and I pulled the meat on that, a quarter at a time, about half a mile, down a path I knew dead-ended at a sheer rock face. Sweat still dripped off my face though I was stripped nearly to bare skin for the first time in months, but with the sled the task at least seemed possible. I thought again of Scott trudging across Antarctica, manhauling all his gear.

At the rock face I stretched a meat pole between two trees. The only access to this cul-de-sac was up Indian Creek. Thick willow and cottonwood saplings formed a wall from that direction, while the cliff blocked every other line of sight. I'd picked this spot a long time ago, thinking of the warden's advice to keep any hunting invisible.

It was when I tried to hoist the meat that I had an idea of its true weight. After taking the slack out of the rope I hefted mightily, and found myself in the air, the meat unmoved, still solidly on the ground. In my winter wool I weighed about two hundred pounds, and the meat didn't budge when I dangled from the rope. If I hadn't been so tired I could have climbed up and down that rope all day.

My books had repeatedly advised freezing meat in the largest pieces possible, discouraging freezer burn, so I struggled all the way with these four enormous quarters. I tried again, running with the rope, trying to jerk the pieces off the ground. But I was like a dog hitting the end of its leash. I stood over the quarters, knowing I'd have to cut them into eighths, just to make them lighter than I was, so I could lift them into the air. I wasn't quite ready to face that.

I peed in a circle around the pile of meat again and shuffled off to bed, with something pulled in my stomach that made it hard to sit up after lying down. For the second straight night I skipped dinner. The feast I'd planned would just have to wait.

I finished the job the next day, finally ending up with eight pieces of meat hanging from the pole. It was frozen now and I stood and looked at the dangling pieces a moment before cutting the inaugural meal. I sawed off a round steak the size of a manhole cover and just as hard. Tucking it under my arm, I slapped at one of the pieces and watched it swing. I laughed.

The steak looked like something out of a Flintstones cartoon—a brontosaurus steak. When my dad and Paul came in they would hardly believe their eyes. I ran my hands down the tenderloins, cuts I'd saved on purpose, since the first night, for the feed I'd put on when they skied into my meadow. We would feast and feast.

In the tent I set the steak next to the stove to thaw and I began to cook. I made a rice pudding that day, and two loaves of bread. Tomorrow was Christmas Eve. I would not let this holiday slip away as I had Thanksgiving. I was going to have a feast all my own. And I was too tired to do anything but cook for the rest of the day.

The steak, propped against the table leg, seemed like an enormous accomplishment. I walked out in the evening with my pipe and before long I wound up at the meat pole. I stared and stared at the chunks of meat swinging from it. I couldn't stop smiling. Though the actual hunt had been ridiculously unplanned and accidental, maybe now I was a mountain man. I had gotten my own food. Even though it'd taken two months, things seemed awfully easy.

10

The thick snow that had been falling all during the moose days gave way to rain on Christmas Eve. Rain made the inside of my tent nearly as damp as outside so there was little point staying cooped up. I carried the moose hide to an open area by the river and stretched it out as widely as I could. It was longer than I was tall, over six feet wide. After cutting four lodgepole pines about ten feet long, I lashed and nailed them into a frame. The timing would be tight, but if at all possible I wanted to have the huge robe tanned and ready for my bed before my brother and father skied in.

I centered the hide in the frame and sat down beside it with a huge ball of string. Taking my Green River mountain man knife, I began punching holes along the hide's border, using a stick of firewood as backing for the knife. I stitched the hide into the frame as I went, my pamphlet on *Brain Tanning the Sioux Way* propped up in the snow next to me. I chuckled over the advice on how much brain to use: "Each animal has enough brains to tan itself."

"Yeah, but what about the tanner?" I wondered.

The point of the knife wore out before I was half done and I continued on with my Buck knife. It wore out before I finished, but it was close, and I tried to make it last. Finally I was pounding on the knife with another stick of firewood, trying to drive it through the tough hide. I was nearly done and I didn't want to take a sharpening break. I'd been cooking Christmas treats like bread and coffee cake all day, and with those steady interruptions it was already nearly dark.

Finally the Buck knife wouldn't do it anymore. I was getting sick of this project, of constantly stopping to retighten all the strings, wanting the hide drum-head tight, of my wool clothes growing thicker and heavier with the rain. I pulled my Swiss army knife from my pocket and its sharply pointed blade went through as if greased. I smiled, thinking I should have been using it all along instead of the large, round-tipped knives.

Its point dulled quickly though and with only a few holes left I was leaning into the knife, putting my weight against it to drive it through. I was kneeling up over the little knife, pressing as hard as I could when I over-balanced and the blade folded back into its closed position, just as it was supposed to, right over my middle finger.

I leapt up in pain and surprise, still holding the knife. I opened my hand but the knife held itself on my finger. When I pulled it away there was a moment of hesitation, the blade gripping bone.

I stomped up to my tent, more mad than hurt, mad that I couldn't have seen that coming, that I'd been such an imbecile. But by the time I reached the tent the amount of blood was a little alarming and I wrapped it tightly and held it in the air awhile. That seemed to do the trick and I went back out to finish the hide. As soon as I dropped my hand down it began to bleed again.

That night, four hours after I'd crushed the blade into my finger, it was still bleeding. I unwrapped it and saw the edges of the cut puckered, pulled away from each other, and knew I should have stitches. I wasn't too excited about giving them to myself, and I wondered if I could if I had to. As a next-to-last resort I used a butterfly bandage to draw the edges together. I finished the bandaging and tied it tight enough to throb.

With the drizzle finally turned to thick, heavy snow, my radio worked well and I held my hand up all evening, checking the finger while I fiddled with the radio. The bleeding really had stopped, I decided, relieved to be able to put away the idea of giving myself stitches.

Soon I picked up a reading of *A Christmas Carol* by Lionel Barrymore and I listened with rapt attention to a story I thought was too tired to ever be interesting again. It really was almost Christmas.

During the night, sometime after I turned off the radio, the sky cleared. When I woke the temperature was zero, my breath forming great steaming clouds while I was still in bed. I whispered, "Merry Christmas."

But the cold made my finger hurt more, and worse yet, once I was out and about, I discovered it had frozen the hide into one gigantic board, supple as a sheet of plywood. I stood staring at it, a day's work gone in stretching it, realizing that it would be impossible to tan with the temperature below freezing. I knew I'd have to cut it down and thaw it, and salt and roll it and bury it in my food cache. I wouldn't have the huge robe until spring, right when I wouldn't need it. And by then I'd no longer have the moose's brain, the essential ingredient in the tanning process. I couldn't imagine a way to save the brain that long.

I started the quick process of taking the hide out of the frame, mad at my heavy mittens for being so hard to work with, mad at having ever stretched it in the first place, mad at everything. When I was trying to haul the frozen hide up the hill to my tent it kept slipping out of my hands and in disgust I pulled off my mittens so I could get a real grip with my bare hands.

By the time I manhandled the hide through the front flap of the tent my fingers had gone through pain to numbness and I stuck them into my armpits and stood beside the stove, having taken just enough time to see that blood had soaked through my new bandage.

When I quit dancing around beside the stove I saw that the finger tips of my right hand were paper white. They stayed that way for a long time. I sat down to read over the first aid for frostbite, wondering if I could manage to pull any more moronic stunts in the next few hours, or if I'd exhausted even my abilities. It was shaping up to be a hell of a Christmas.

That afternoon, after I thawed my fingers and the hide, and I'd finished salting and storing it, I hiked up to the top of Indian Ridge.

Three thousand feet above my tent I was able to see the sun again. I took several deep breaths, trying to relax, trying to put the rush of the moose kill and the foolishness of the robe behind me.

Sitting in a snowdrift, I watched the sun set, reddening the few clouds and the endless stretches of snowed-over peaks and ridges. I pictured my family warm at home, opening all their carefully wrapped gifts, and I grinned, imagining the looks on their faces as they passed my presents around. I hoped they'd realize they were jokes, just a way to show I hadn't forgotten, but suddenly I wasn't as sure as I'd been when I packed them. They really were some pretty stupid things.

But it felt good to be out in the open again and I stayed up there until nearly dusk, trying not to think of anything at all. I unwrapped my finger and found that the cut had closed nicely. Maybe things were looking up. Sitting in the snowdrift, I rebandaged my finger, making it pretty, then I hurried back down to get home before the night grew completely black.

For my Christmas celebration I cooked mashed potatoes, canned corn, and enough moose steak to completely fill a frying pan top to bottom, side to side. When I was done I pushed back from the table as grossly stuffed as I would be at home and I smiled, thinking how in Milwaukee they'd all be doing the same thing. But tomorrow Paul and Dad would be climbing into the station wagon, beginning their drive out to Montana. The drive would take two days, and by the twenty-eighth they should be starting their ski.

I spent those two days in a flurry of cleaning and cooking. I cooked and cooked until my little table was stacked with crisp brown loaves of bread and coffee cakes and rice puddings and everything else I'd learned to make and had grown to think was pretty deluxe. I filled the water buckets, having to chop through the new layer of ice the cold had coated over my watering hole in Indian Creek. I even mixed a jug full of the lemonade mix I hoarded jealously. The only thing I had to drink other than straight water, I hadn't brought in nearly enough. It was a special occasion drink. I made an entire gallon.

That night I put my biggest pot on and stoked the stove until the sides glowed red. Though it was dropping down somewhere near zero outside, the temperature in my tent was pushing ninety when, an hour later, the water in the pot was hot enough to steam. For the first time since my near disastrous last drive to Magruder a month ago, I took off all my clothes.

I stepped into a galvanized wash tub and with a pitcher I began to scoop the hot water over my head. I washed my hair quickly, using the water draining down my body to clean the rest of me as best I could. I only had a couple gallons of hot water for my entire bath, and I wound up cutting it with cold, just to have enough to rinse with. The whole process was hurried and cramped, less than enjoyable.

But afterward, drying off naked and clean, finally free of the press of layer upon layer of wool, I giggled at just how good it felt. Even with the roaring stove though, ice still clung to the floor by the door, and drafts swirled through the tent. I put off dressing as long as I could, but eventually slipped on a clean union suit and crawled between the covers.

Finally, on the twenty-eighth, when I couldn't do anything else to prepare for my first visitors, I decided to hike down to Magruder to meet them, knowing I wouldn't be able just to sit in my tent and wait. The channel was completely frozen over now, the snow a blanket of insulation for the water running underneath, and after cleaning every hint of ice from the waterfall at the end, I was sure it would be all right for a night on its own. I threw on my pack, with its usual load of rough first-aid gear, clothes, food, and sleeping bag, and headed upriver.

At Raven Creek, two miles from my tent, the usual turning point of my nightly strolls, I had to put on the snowshoes I'd strapped to the pack. Once my well-packed trail gave out I was into four feet of snow, and I couldn't go on without the shoes.

Halfway to Magruder I flushed a grouse from the brush beside the river and it launched across the Selway, landing in the thick woods on the other side. In just the week since I'd shot the moose the river had finished freezing over, had even been covered by a foot of snow, and I crossed after the grouse without having to think about breaking through. It was already a little hard to believe I'd been so concerned about it before.

The grouse played a game of hide-and-seek with me for nearly an hour, but I eventually caught it sneaking along a branch and shot off its head. Boone retrieved it for me perfectly, dropping it at my feet, and I grinned hugely. With everything going this smoothly I could nearly pretend the whole moose hide debacle had never happened. Without the blood-tinged bandage still wrapped around my finger, I might have tried.

I picked up the grouse and tied it to my pack, wishing this had happened on the way back, when Paul and Dad could see it all. I hoped we'd bounce out another on our way to the tent, the three of us together, that I'd finally be able to share all of this with somebody.

At this moment, I thought, they were up somewhere near the pass, probably over it by now, shushing down the long drops toward the Selway. They couldn't have had a better day for it. Low twenties, sunny, the world so bright it hurt.

The night before, during a quick run through the radio stations (a pretty much useless attempt with the clear skies), I'd caught a scrap of a Boise weather report saying they expected temperatures of ten below the next night. I'd learned it was usually ten or fifteen degrees colder here than in Boise. If that was really headed this way I hoped Paul and Dad had heard about it, that they'd make good time while the weather was good.

I crossed back over the thick ice and snow blanket on the Selway and headed on, deciding we'd spend the first night in the solid log house at Magruder. I'd cook them a true-blue grouse dinner while they told heroic tales of their trip.

I didn't reach Magruder until nearly dark, cutting my safety rule about being wherever I was going while there was still light unusually close for the second time in just a few days. At the signboard pointing toward the station I left a note, written with the lead tip of one of my

.22 rounds, letting Dad and Paul know I was at the ranger station. That'd cut ten miles off their trail and I was confident I would see them the next day.

I hurried the last half mile to Magruder and in the dark I found that someone—it must have been the wardens—had misplaced the key to the ranger station. Digging my headlamp out of my pack, I scrounged through the outbuildings until I found a bolt cutter and then cut my way in.

I built up the fire and opened the propane lines. I wasn't sure how long we'd be here, so I left the water off. The last thing I wanted to do was break a water line. Once the fire had taken hold in the furnace and the house had begun to warm I cranked the handle around on the old phone. Two long, one short—the signal for West Fork Ranger Station, over the pass in Montana.

The ranger told me Dad and Paul had stopped by early that morning and were on their way in. He also said they expected it to drop down to fifteen below tonight. He asked what kind of skiers they were, what kind of experience they had with this kind of thing. I doubted they had any, but I told him they'd be all right. Until a few months ago I hadn't had any experience with anything either, and I was all right.

After I hung up I got out my map and studied their route yet again. The ranger had told me the road was plowed farther than I'd guessed. They only had twenty-five miles to go—ten to the pass and fifteen down to here. I stepped out on the porch, and it didn't seem that cold to me.

Stepping back into the toasty cabin, I made a quick meal of canned stew, saving the grouse for them tomorrow. I crawled into bed then, listening to the mice growing active in the sudden heat, thinking of Paul and Dad tented up out there somewhere in the blackness toward Montana. Maybe in the morning I'd walk on up that way. Maybe I could even get another grouse or two, so we could have a real welcome-in feed.

In the dark of the cabin I grinned, picturing it all.

11

I slept in a little the next morning, then got up in a hurry, imagining my father and Paul skiing in to find me snoozing away in this fancy lodge. Not a very mountain manly picture. I rushed through a quick breakfast—nothing more than a cup of coffee and a piece of bread—and started out to meet them.

In my rush, it took a few moments to realize how surprising the cold was. I stopped in the center of the cabin's meadow and glanced up into the pale, ice-blue sky. Lifting my head let the air slip in around my throat and I quickly pulled myself deeper into my coat. I pushed hard up the hill to the main road and by the time I turned up it, following Deep Creek toward the pass, I'd begun to warm up.

There were no ski trails in the clean snow, only the old, snow-covered dent of the last snow machine track, and I followed that, sinking in less than I would in the powder. I hadn't walked half an hour before I began craning my neck around the bends, to see them that much faster. A big grin hung on my mouth. They wouldn't believe their eyes when I popped around the corner.

I started out with a pack full of stuff I didn't need and the more I thought about it the heavier it seemed. It was full of the same things it held yesterday, things that would only be necessary if something bad happened. Walking along, waiting to see them any second, I wondered why I bothered bringing it all, and I stopped just long enough to leave my pack at the side of the road. I left my big down coat there too. Going uphill I'd be plenty warm without it.

I pushed on alone, my grin growing bigger at each turn, picturing the surprise on their faces, but at each turn I only saw yet another barren stretch of snow-covered road and snow-covered creek and snow-covered trees. My grin faded each time, but never quite went away. I'd need it at the next turn.

I walked for quite a while before I felt the cold. I started walking faster, waiting for the warmth to come, waiting to see the skiers moving darkly against the white world before me. Then I walked faster still, without touching the cold.

Finally, after only three miles or so, I had to turn around. I'd never felt anything like this cold. My pack and coat were a couple of miles away and suddenly that distance was frightening. I took just enough time to make a sign in the snow out of sticks, telling them I was at Magruder. Then I stood a moment more, arms wrapped around my chest, looking up the road, trying to will them to turn the corner before I had to walk away from them.

But they didn't turn that corner and when I started back toward Magruder I walked as fast as possible, clumsy in the snowshoes. Even that pace didn't help me warm up.

Shuffling through the powdery snow, I suddenly wondered if I'd make it to my coat. My chest was cold now, not just my hands and feet and face. Cold under my shirts and long johns, cold like iron. I knew enough about hypothermia to know I'd made a serious mistake leaving my coat and I stumbled back down my trail, trying to hurry, now looking around each bend for my pack and coat, rather than for my dad and brother. I could not quite recall where I'd left them.

Then, when I was running more from panic than sense, I turned a corner and saw the pack. I squirmed into the coat, which was even colder than I was, and continued to run until I felt heat under the heavy down. When I reached the ranger station I was exhausted. I'd covered all of six miles.

I fired up the wood furnace and, after warming through and

through and getting my breath back, I thought of how much less exciting it would be to sit here and wait for them to show up, rather than meeting them up there someplace in the snow. But the thought of the cold still made me shiver and I snowshoed out to the weather station in the meadow and read the maximum and minimum thermometers. Maximum had been six below, minimum, last night, thirty-two below.

Instead of thinking grand thoughts of the reunion I began to think just of my father and brother, up there somewhere toward the pass, the cold stiffening their fingers, their legs, their very thoughts, the same way it had mine. It had to be even colder up there. I wondered what it was doing to them.

I sat in the ranger station, looking out the windows, stoking the furnace to have the house crackling hot when they arrived. But they did not show up all that day or evening. After dark I cranked up the phone to West Fork. The ranger whose dinner I interrupted told me this weather must have caught them halfway. It had been in the twenties when they left. He guessed they were holed up at Blondie's, the old trapper's cabin, waiting for the weather to break.

Blondie's was a crumbling cabin built fifty years before. Blondie himself had frozen to death in a blizzard that caught him trying to hike out to the Bitterroot Valley for Thanksgiving. I checked my map again and found that the cabin was only a few miles from the top of the pass, about twelve or thirteen miles from Magruder. If that's as far as they were they hadn't got far. And I knew they wouldn't stop, wouldn't hole up. They'd keep crushing on. Movement would seem the only option in cold like this. Sitting still would just seem to make the misery last longer.

After hanging up the phone, I went straight to bed. In the morning I wasn't going to stop until I found them.

It was still pitch black in the ranger station when I woke and went to the door to check the weather. The sky was close enough and clear enough it seemed as if the stars were within reach. But I didn't reach.

The stars looked like the very heart of ice—as if they could steal the last trace of heat left in anything alive.

I had not left the porch and my nose had already stuck together and the skin all across my face had tightened and shrunk away from the cold. I wondered what in the world it could be like up at the pass, three thousand feet closer to those stars.

Hurrying back into the cabin, I put as much wood into the furnace as possible, kicking the last piece in until I could shut the door. I made pancakes for breakfast, feeding them to Boone until she lost interest, then cooking an extra twenty for road food, stuffing them into the front pockets of my down coat. I strapped my snowshoes on in the living room rather than outside, where the cold would numb my fingers long before I could cinch the buckles.

I threw on my pack, full of emergency gear, and closed the cabin door behind me. The flattened snow on the porch squeaked outrageously in the frozen air. By the time I reached the main road the sky toward the pass was beginning to pale, and I climbed toward that lightness.

The snow crunched and squeaked under my snowshoes and in the frigid, empty air I could hear every swish of wool, every creak of leather from my boots and snowshoe bindings. The snowshoeing was not hard. For the first three miles I was in yesterday's trail. After that I was in the old snowmobile trail, which had about a half a foot of fresh snow in it. While staring down at my feet I kicked four moose out of the creekbottom. Their crashing run through the willows startled me.

It was fully light by the time I was breaking new trail, the sky the pale, washed-out blue of winter. I passed the landmarks I knew on the bottom from when I'd driven through here in the early desperate weeks—creeks mostly: Cache Creek, Cactus, Gabe, and Scimitar.

Until then I'd been climbing slowly, but after passing the land line phone box at Hell's Half Acre, I began the real climb to the pass. It was late, pushing noon, and though in the morning I'd forced myself not to expect them at every bend, I couldn't keep myself from it now. I was only four or five miles from Blondie's and they'd have to have been up and moving for quite some time by now, easily skiing those five miles down while I'd snowshoed eight miles up. I began to peek around every corner again, holding my breath until another empty section of frozen road stretched out before me.

It had been thirty-six below when I left Magruder and I couldn't imagine where they were or what had happened to them. I tried to picture spending last night in a stoveless backpacking tent, or a collapsing log cabin, but I couldn't do it. For me the day's cold wasn't anything like yesterday's, not with my coat. My beard and the front of my hat and scarf were all caked with ice, but the going was just hard enough to keep me fairly comfortable. I had no idea what kind of clothing they had on, and I knew they had never been in cold like this before. Neither had I.

I passed Halfway Creek and Pete Creek. The sun on the snow was dazzling. The entire world sparkled silently. Occasional breezes sent glistening cascades from the tree branches, but it was mostly still. I made the only noise out here. Up this high there weren't even any animal tracks.

At one o'clock it was time to turn around to ensure getting back before dark. But there was still no trace of them. I looked up the trail, at the untracked snow, and back down my snowshoe track, where I should be going. I held a few pancakes under my coat until they'd thawed partially and then ate them. They were less than delicious. I dropped more to Boone and she broke them up and swallowed them frozen.

I couldn't imagine them not getting this far, not unless something bad had happened, and I decided to keep going a little farther, keep going until I found some sort of sign.

Around the next bend, not two hundred yards from where I had rested, I saw ski tracks. I ran up the hill and shouted, thinking they must be right here someplace. But the tracks only came this far and turned silently around, back up the hill. I kept running up the tracks, shouting now and then. I had to be right on top of them now.

That they'd turned around where they did didn't make me feel too good. It didn't make sense. I remembered a couple of shacks at Slow Gulch, a half a mile or so up the road. Maybe they'd holed up there. But why would they ski down a half mile and turn around? I was wondering about frostbite or twisted ankles or about my fifty-three-year-old dad's infamous back going out on him. Or of Paul, who could turn the simplest descent of a staircase into a leg fracture.

And about hypothermia, what they used to call exposure. That was worst of all. Why would they come here and turn around, after two nights out? It didn't make any sense. That's how hypothermic people acted toward the end, when the cold chilled their brains. I made time getting up to those cabins, the snow flying away from my snowshoes, covering the tracks of their skis, the rhythm of my breathing falling into time with the chugging pump of my legs.

When the shacks at Slow Gulch were in sight the ski trails broke from the road, sinking through the snow-covered willows to the shacks. Running, I started shouting again, excited to finally see them.

But no shouts answered mine. I broke through the snow over a willow and had to swim out of the hole, one leg on the surface, the other buried to my waist. I shouted again, and there was still no answer. Looking to those two buildings as I struggled free of the hole in the snow, I wondered what was waiting in them for me. Back on my feet I ran again.

I burst through the door of the first cabin and it was empty. I stared into the dark interior, my eyes still squinting against the spectacular glare of the snow. Trying to slow down my breathing, I walked out of the cabin. The place was crisscrossed with ski tracks, but none had gone into this cabin. If I had been thinking I wouldn't have gone in either. Then I turned to the second cabin and really didn't want to know what was inside. All the tracks went into it.

Pushing aside the images of the frozen bodies at Wounded Knee and the Scott party in Antarctica, I pushed the door open. It was half full of hay and I was glad that was all there was in it. I could see a few traces of their presence, but no fire.

Slowly I began to trace their trails throughout the shack area. I found the spot they'd used for a latrine. I found everything they had done here, except their fire. They had not built a fire. It was forty below and they hadn't built a fire. I followed every track they'd made, unable to believe they hadn't built a fire. They must have been out of their heads with the cold.

I circled around the camp once more and then went back to the road, following their freshest trail. It led up toward the pass. I trudged along in their tracks, still shouting now and then, but no longer believing I was right behind them, and no longer thinking they were simply late. I wondered if they had left for the stouter cabin at Blondie's. The rendezvous had turned into something feeling a lot more like a rescue.

When I came to Kerlee Creek I saw where they had skied over to the signpost and kicked the snow off the sign. I felt almost sick, picturing them wondering where they were, wondering how far they had come and how far they had to go and how long these hellish temperatures would last. I shouted again and the sound echoed back to me.

Just past Kerlee Creek there was a series of ski pole circles stamped into the snow, spelling out 9:30. I was five hours behind them. I didn't shout again. I kept going up to Blondie's.

Why would they stomp out times? Only if they thought somebody else would be up here. They'd only think that if they thought somebody would be looking for them. And they'd only think people were looking for them if they were in trouble.

They hadn't left the road at Blondie's, on the way in or the way out. I kept going, but it was obvious now they were going for the other side. I hesitated. There was no way I was going to get back to Magruder before dark. Going the other way they had a five-hour head start on me, and I'd already gone twelve miles. There was little chance of my catching them. If they were in desperate shape the way to get to them would be from the other side. I thought of the phone box at Hell's Half. It was on the same line as the Magruder phone, so it should work. I wanted to see them more than I'd wanted most

things in my life, but it would be safest for them if I got back to that
phone and got some Forest Service guys heading up the other side.

I stopped on the snow-covered road, a couple of miles shy of the
summit, and tried to collect myself before moving on. My legs were
feeling the climb and I was getting cold. I thought soup sounded like
a good idea, but I couldn't take the time to build a fire. I knew going
back the way I came, alone, knowing there wasn't going to be any
reunion, knowing there would be no one around the next bend, was
going to be harder than the climb up. Frozen pancakes weren't going
to be enough fuel.

I got out my backpack stove and poured gasoline over it and lit
the gasoline, trying to warm the stove up enough to work, but it was
hopeless. I put the stove and the soup packet back in my pack and
started for Hell's Half, eating more pancakes as I went, thawing them
under my arms.

It was almost worse passing all their landmarks a second time,
knowing I was getting farther from them this time instead of closer.
The snow kicked off that sign and the time stamped in the snow were
two of the most pathetic things I had ever seen. I kept straight past
Slow Gulch and still could not believe they had not built a fire. Their
nights without a fire must have lasted forever. It was dark then from
five in the evening until eight in the morning. Fifteen hours of silent
darkness fighting to stay warm. I kept pressing my tired legs toward
the phone box.

I reached it with an hour of light left. The ranger I talked to
said, no, they hadn't heard from them, but he'd take a drive up and
see if their car was still at the trail head. He asked again where I was
and suggested getting my ass to Magruder. It was cold out, he said. I
said thanks and told him I would call again from Magruder.

Magruder was eight miles away now. Disappointment and anxi-
ety were mixing with the exertion and the cold, wearing me out. I
shuffled on, pausing once to crunch over to Deep Creek for a drink.
There was a hole open in the ice about a yard wide. I was reaching
my cup to it when the ice gave way.

The creek was very small, but I couldn't get back to shore before one of my shoes dipped in. The rawhide webbing was instantly fogged with ice. Realizing I hadn't fallen into the water, I sank back in the snow to give my heart a chance to slow. Then I got my drink and crippled back to the road.

With the ice the one snowshoe seemed weighted with lead. I couldn't break it off with anything. I took both of the snowshoes off and tested the road. The packed snow machine trail seemed to hold my weight fairly well and I strapped my snowshoes onto my backpack and kept walking. I only broke through the crusted trail a few times, but each of those jarring steps seemed to drive my leg through my hip, and the extra effort of pulling myself out of the hole hardly seemed worth it.

In the last trace of even the dusky light I passed the sign I had made with sticks in the snow the day before. I stared at it a moment, then kicked it out, knowing no one would read it now.

I had three miles to go and I plodded on slowly in the darkness. When I entered the thicker trees around the road even the starlight was blotted, and I started to wander off the snowmobile track, floundering up to my hips in the snow. I stopped long enough to get my headlamp out of my pack and strap it onto my chest, its metal backing too cold to put on my head.

The second wind I waited for never came. I was beat, and the snowshoes on my pack were heavy with ice. The flashlight batteries waned and I was shocked breathless when something broke through the brush by the creek and leapt onto the road. The light picked out a shape darker than the darkness, loping down the trail in front of me— one of the moose I had seen that morning. I could hear it trotting in front of me a few more times, but never saw it again.

I hit the Selway at 6:30 and turned up it for the last half mile to Magruder. The cabin was dark against the starlit snowfield. I was as alone as I had been since my first days in here. I pushed the door open and lit one of the propane lamps. There was half an inch of frost on the front of my hat and down my coat to my chest. It cracked and fell on the pine floor when I undressed.

I looked at the phone and then went into the basement and restocked the furnace. After putting some water on the stove to heat, I went to the phone box and turned the crank. Two long, one short.

A ranger answered the phone quickly and told me my dad and brother had made it out half an hour before, minutes before I'd reached Magruder. The ranger said he'd arranged for them to come back at ten the next morning and call me. I thanked him and hung up.

My exhaustion disappeared. I nearly danced around the gloomy cabin on my played-out legs. I had a small party, extravagantly lighting the rest of the lamps and cooking another can of stew I found in the basement. For dessert I had hot chocolate and a can of fruit cocktail taken with the stew.

It wasn't until I was in the darkness again, in bed, that I thought about the collapse of my Christmas plans. My tent was full of frozen bread and coffee cake and rice pudding, all I had made to feast with my first guests. All that and the fifty miles I had covered were for naught. I wasn't going to see anything of my family other than a few miles of five-hour-old ski tracks. The sleep that I thought would take me in seconds was a long time in coming that night.

The next morning I cleaned the cabin and shut down the propane and everything else. The minimum thermometer read forty below. At ten o'clock sharp I cranked the phone for West Fork and the ranger put my dad and brother on the two available lines. I was so giddy to hear their voices, to actually be talking to them after the horrible images that had flashed through my brain as I approached the cabins at Slow Gulch, that I had trouble controlling my voice.

I first asked if they were all right, and my dad told me he'd frost-bit a handful of his fingers, but other than that they were fine.

They'd spent the first night on the pass, making only nine miles. I could hardly believe they'd let themselves stay there—it had to be minus forty or worse that high—but when they'd reached it it had seemed like a destination, something accomplished, and they'd decided to stay.

The cold hit that night and it made everything take longer; they hadn't gotten on the trail until 10:30 the next morning. The snow-mobile path gave them fits, my father said, their skis sliding off into the runner tracks and riding on their sides, turning their ankles. The downhill that they had expected to be one push and a fifteen-mile glide had turned out to be hardly easier than the climb to the pass. My dad said the snow had the characteristics of sand—and he had never seen anything like it in Wisconsin.

When they saw the cabins at Slow Gulch they couldn't resist. They'd gone on a little farther and then turned back for the cabins, thinking they might continue on in the morning. About four miles the second day.

They didn't know I was at Magruder, and with the cold they'd eaten their food faster than they expected and didn't know how much extra I had to feed them while they were in. They were worried they'd put me in a bind, eating food I'd need later in the year. And here I sat with a whole moose.

I finally had to ask about the fire. Why no fire? They told me they hadn't built one because they were afraid of melting everything and getting wet besides.

The third morning my dad's fingers were frozen; he was down to having Paul zip his clothes for him, and they knew they had to give up. He had been ready before Paul and he was too cold to stand still. So he left without him and stamped the times in the snow to let Paul know how far behind he was. They made it out that day, thirteen miles. It would have been eleven to Magruder.

We didn't talk long, but the brief flashes he gave me of their journey made me feel even worse for them than I had when I saw the snow knocked off the sign at Kerlee Creek. He told about nearly crying when Paul, wearing his huge mittens, knocked the pan full of bacon grease off their little stove and into the snow. They'd been burning calories like mad and he'd been planning on frying bread in the grease. He had been so counting on that hot grease, he said. And when they got back to the car at dark it would not start and he said he sat behind the wheel, perfectly ready to give up.

But Paul put the camp stove under the oil pan until the car started and they stopped at West Fork and found out how close I had been. They felt bad for letting me down, Paul said, and I thought of him zipping our father into his clothes, then chasing him through these foreign, snowbound mountains.

We said good luck to each other and had to hang up.

It was a long ten miles back to Indian Creek that day. The channel was fine, despite the temperatures. I chopped out a little ice, and went back to my tent.

It took three days to thaw out my plastic five-gallon water jug and I nearly melted through its side, but caught it just as the plastic began to bubble. The cold snap took a little longer to give up. And it was longer still before I could think of their desperate attempt to visit without my throat getting tight and dry. I knew how my father had felt watching that bacon grease steam its way down through the snow and disappear when he had already known how it would taste.

I knew exactly how he felt.

12

During the long walk back from Magruder I'd expected to reel into a depression after the failure of the visit, but that never really happened. The days thawing my tent were slow; full of small chores and fire tending, reading and cooking. I was tired, and the slow pace was nice.

The second afternoon back I went to my food cache to retrieve some potatoes for dinner. Elk tracks were thick throughout the meadow, but I was surprised to find them in the timber so near my tent. As I got closer to the cache the ground grew more trampled, and soon I saw bits of hay scattered through the snow. The hay the hunters had given to me to insulate my cache.

The cache was a mess. Driven down by temperatures perhaps, or emboldened by my absence, the elk had eaten all the hay. They'd also broken through some of the old planks of the roof, and pushed others aside with their hooves.

My cache had lain open to the air at thirty below zero. I lay down to reach into the potatoes and found burst cans of corn and peas. The carrots were frost-covered sticks. The potatoes seemed like potatoes, though, and I carried a bag into my tent. By the next morning they thawed, turning black and oozing the vilest reeking goo I'd ever smelled.

I threw the potatoes out and salvaged the cans that hadn't broken, bringing them into my tent. I repaired the cache, but I was down to mash potato buds and half the cans I'd had days before. *The Big Sky* characters were always saying a man could survive on nothing but meat. It seemed a mountain man type of thing to do, and I didn't feel as badly about the losses as I should have.

The next day, while lazing around on my bed, cooking one of the cake mixes my sister Ellen had sent in, I suddenly heard snow machines and I stepped out in time to meet the lion hunters from Paradise. They invited me to stop down anytime and they roared off. For the next few days I heard their machines going by twice a day as they cruised the river, looking for lion crossings, but they didn't bother pulling up to my tent often.

Once the tent was thawed I took a hike up to the top of Indian Ridge to get into the sun again. The weather was still clear and cold and sitting on top of the ridge, I pulled out the moose ribs I'd brought for lunch, only to find they were frozen solid. Sunning in the five-degree air, I whittled tiny slivers of frozen meat, holding them in my mouth until they were soft enough to chew. When most of the meat was gone I gave the bones to Boone, who lay in the snow chewing noisily. As usual I stayed in the sun as long as I could before dropping back down into the dark river cut that was home.

On the way down I crossed a track I hadn't seen before. I followed until it crossed a crusted-over drift. In the hard snow I was able to see more than just the broken line of a trail in deep snow—I was able to see paw prints. I stood stunned, staring at the first mountain lion tracks I'd ever seen. The feet were much bigger than I expected, four or five inches, roundish like any house cat's. I smiled looking at them, and when the lion hunters next stopped by my tent I did not tell them about the lion on the ridge.

The cold held on and on: negative teens or twenties at night, rising only to single digits during the day. Every night was a battle, wondering if it would be better to leave my head out to freeze or to tuck it in under the blankets, where my nose would wrestle with my once-a-month-bath aromas. I slept with a watch cap on. By morning the ice of my breaths edged the blankets, laying snaking fingers of cold around my neck.

The wood stove I'd been given was an old one, and a cheap one, its sides too thin and its dampers too crude to hold heat long. I could have gotten up every couple of hours to restoke it, but watching its sides glow red with the fire inside, I wasn't very comfortable about sleeping with it going and I decided to suffer through the cold. By dawn it would be below zero inside and I knew my rubber-soled boots would be frozen, that I'd have to stamp on them just to straighten them enough to get my feet into them. Every morning I lay in bed until last night's tea finally forced me through the tent flap in a clothes-unbuttoning rush.

Then I'd stoke up the stove and set on the percolator and walk down to the channel, wiggling my toes in my frozen boots. I chopped ice every morning, even the waterfall at the end of the channel freezing solid every night. By the time I was back at the tent my face and chest would be frosted over from my breath and I'd unzip my coat and take off my boots to let the stove's heat engulf me. The coffee would be ready by then and I'd sit and sip, waiting for my oatmeal to cook, reading everything my father and sister had sent in.

The wardens were due in at the middle of the month and I decided to take a walk down to Paradise to see if that phone worked. If it did I'd call out and ask if they knew exactly when they'd be coming in. Every morning, stamping on my frozen boots, I thought of the biologist's offer of a week trade-off in here. I thought of what it would be like to be out again, to have a thermostat, to wake up warm, to see all my friends again. I'd ask the Forest Service guys if they'd heard any word from the biologist.

But on the ninth of January the cold broke. It hit thirty-two that day and instead of hiking down to Paradise I walked up Indian Creek to the meat pole. I'd been stuffing myself with moose meat every night, and cooking huge steaks to slice into sandwich meat for every lunch, but there were still three untouched quarters hanging from the pole, and almost half the fourth. If the weather stayed warm for long the meat would go bad. I pushed at a rock-hard quarter and watched it swing, trying to decide what to do.

I walked slowly back to my tent and spent the day reading my manuals, studying curing methods. I didn't have a smokehouse, and I didn't have brine barrels. Angier suggested cutting the meat into chunks as big as was manageable and rubbing them in a mix of salt and spice. No matter the method, it'd require bringing the meat into the tent and working with it for days. I couldn't do that, not with the wardens due in. I wondered if I'd be able to bring myself to bury it, waste it all. Somehow I forgot it was still January.

The next morning the tent was darker than it should have been and, blowing through the door for my usual emergency pee, I stepped into a blizzard. It was still warm, but safely warm—in the twenties—and I stopped worrying about the moose. I hiked the six miles to Paradise through wildly flying snow.

At one exposed bend of the river, where the wind had cleared the ice of all but the newest snow, I saw the trail of an elk that had run down the mountain and crossed the river. Its tracks showed how it leaped the last bit of riverbank, landing on what looked exactly like more snow. But on the ice, all hell had broken loose. The elk's front feet had shot to the left, while his back legs had done the splits. He held on for what must have been a long time, his feet making wild looping patterns on the ice, but then the snow had been wiped clean by the big broad side of the elk spinning over the ice.

I laughed, translating what must have occurred, and I wished I'd been just a few minutes earlier, that I could have seen the mighty, majestic elk take such a pratfall.

Walking on, though, I thought of what a fragile thread held everything together out here. If the elk had broken something, dislocated a hip (which looked more probable than not), it would have been all over. There would have been nothing left but a ring of dirty snow and a pile of stomach grass centered in a haze of coyote tracks.

Since the river had frozen over I'd found a number of coyote kills. The coyotes, working together in groups of six or seven, would drive deer out of the timber and onto the flat, level bed of the river. Tufts of hair would show where the coyotes had nipped, how they'd weakened the prey.

Occasionally there'd be tiny, sparkling bright drops of blood in the trail. I always expected a gradual progression, more hair, more blood, then more, and finally the kill. But it never went like that. Always just a little hair, sometimes no blood, and then, suddenly, the huge, trampled circle, with nothing but the stain and the grass. Only once did I see a spot where a deer had fallen but regained its feet and run on. Its final circle was just yards off.

I thought of my parents, months ago, wondering what I'd do if I chopped off my foot with an ax. If I'd known, I could have described the way the coyote tracks would flatten the entire area around the end.

Once at Paradise I called out to West Fork. Since the phone at Indian Creek had never worked I was pretty sure a tree had clipped the line between there and Magruder, so I was surprised to hear a ranger pick up the phone over in Montana. They told me the warden was due in on the fifteenth. They hadn't heard anything about the biologist or his plan of taking my place for a few days.

There really wasn't much else to do at Paradise so I turned back around. They'd only said they hadn't heard about the biologist's idea, I told myself, not that it wasn't going to happen. I planned on getting myself ready for it, packing just in case he should come in ready to relieve me.

I'd only made it a few hundred yards when the Paradise mountain lion guide, Brian, the same one I'd met in the fall, came barreling down the river on his rickety old snow machine. While out trailing a bobcat, he told me, he'd lost his newest hound. That'd been last week, but he asked me to keep my eyes peeled.

I thought of the endless series of ridges and peaks surrounding us forever, heavy timber clotting every draw, and I tried to imagine a hound surviving out there alone for more than a day or two. But I thought of what it would be like to have Boone suddenly disappear, and I told him I'd look around.

Brian wasn't a big talker so we stood around looking out at the frozen stretch of river and eventually I said something about heading back before dark. He surprised me by inviting me to stay at Paradise for the night. I climbed onto the back of his little machine and we roared off, Boone giving wild chase.

The outfitter tent we stayed in—the same one I shared drinks in at the end of the big-game season, the one the old man left to drive into the ditch—was musty and cold, but Brian had the fire going quickly and I sat down to look at all the things they had. Cabinets and shelves lined the walls, full of all sorts of bottles and cooking ingredients and tools. The cooking stove and the lighting were powered by propane, which seemed a nearly unimaginable luxury. I thought of my little tent, packed with nothing but clothes, dog food and mice. I felt like I was in a real house again.

Brian took off his coat and his shoulder holster with its .45 caliber six-shooter. In the fall I'd learned to ask about guns and Brian showed this one to me. It was heavy and looked like something out of a Western.

I followed him around while he fed the lion hounds. They slept in hay-lined fifty-five-gallon drums buried horizontally in the hillside, the earth's heat warming them the same way it'd kept the food in my cache from freezing. The hounds stood outside the drums to eat, held in place by heavy chain leashes. Brian told me Boone could take the drum his dog had been using.

I knew these guys didn't have pets and I knew dogs had no place in their tents. I wondered how Boone would take it. I'd made a collar for her a while back, just to get her used to the idea, thinking ahead to when we'd be out in the world. We stood in front of the empty drum and I snapped the chain onto her collar. Brian put an extra bowl of food in front of her but it wasn't what she was used to, and she only sniffed. As we walked away, toward the big tent, she began to whine. When we'd disappeared inside she began to bark. And to howl. And to plead.

She kept at it so long Brian was moved to explain that he'd let

her come in, but some of the clients might be allergic to dog hair, so
he thought it'd be better to leave her out. It was fully night now and
I couldn't even think of walking back to Indian Creek.

We spent the night playing cribbage, something I hadn't done
since high school. We sipped a little whiskey too, and Brian nearly
became talkative. He was probably only a few years older than I, the
closest person to my age I'd met in here yet.

Boone cried and whimpered the entire time. I felt sorry for her,
but underneath that I felt a tingle of embarrassment. Brian's dogs
weren't making a peep. I wondered if Boone would have the sense to
crawl into the drum for warmth. Just before I crawled into one of the
empty hunter bunks I walked out to check on her. She was inside,
whining quietly, and I snuck away before she could know I was there.
The last thing I wanted was a renewed round of howling to listen to
as I lay in the strange bed.

By morning Boone was standing outside the drum, waiting for me.
When the chain was unsnapped she bolted away, then turned in a
spray of snow and came back, leaping up on me as if some horrible
mishap had separated us, as if I hadn't hooked her onto the chain
myself. Brian shook his head, but smiled.

He offered a ride to Indian Creek, since he was heading that
way himself, looking for cat sign. He loaded a trailer box with a pair
of hounds and we rumbled off slowly, Boone trotting anxiously
behind, always keeping me in sight.

Before we reached Indian Creek we bumped into another set of
hunters, this one based up at Magruder Crossing, about six miles
upstream of my tent. Cary was the dog owner and Phil rode behind
him, smiling a lot, looking as sure about most of this stuff as I did. He
talked with some sort of an Eastern accent and I guessed he was a
client, but Cary introduced him as a friend.

Brian and I'd been stopped when they pulled into view, dragging
their own box full of dogs. Brian was looking up the draw across the
river, studying ravens through his binoculars. "Kill?" Cary asked.

Brian shrugged and they decided it was worth checking out. They asked if I wanted to go with them, to hike up the mountain after the dogs, hoping we'd find a lion kill and be able to track the lion straight from it. I'd never seen a mountain lion before and said, "Sure."

Cary had me hold Boone back while they let the hounds out and chained them up. He explained that they weren't very good with strange dogs. Once they were ready, the hounds all on leads, they told me to lock Boone into the trailer box and we'd be off. I didn't want to do that to Boone again so soon, but they told me that the hounds might turn on her and kill her. I didn't want to back out in front of these guys, mountain lion hunters of all people, at least not because I felt sorry for a dog.

I could feel them looking at me. They said the ravens were close and it would probably only be an hour. I put Boone in the box.

As we started snowshoeing away Boone began her racket again, as if she'd never let up from the night before. Two miles away, up on the mountain, when we stood still for a rest, the sound of her moans floated up to us. I avoided the eyes of the hunters and wished she'd just shut up.

We never did find a kill, or even see the ravens again, once we were up there, and we were back to the machines in little over an hour. Since Cary had already checked the river upstream, Brian decided he'd call it a day and we split up. Cary couldn't take another rider, and Brian offered to take me home but I told them all I'd be happy to walk.

I waited by the river, holding on to Boone while the snow machines rumbled off in opposite directions. When I couldn't hear their whining scream I thumped Boone on the side and scratched her ears and we headed home together.

For the next week I saw Brian and Cary and Phil nearly every day. I started eating after dark, sawing steaks from the meat pole by headlamp, not wanting even these guys to know about my food source. At one point Brian talked a little too much about moose and I had a nervous feeling that he knew, that he was hinting around, seeing how much I'd admit. But the next day he brought over the front quarter of a deer. He said he couldn't imagine going without meat for so long.

He said, smiling, that the deer was left over from the season, which seemed like an awfully thin veneer over the truth. He seemed to be leaving himself open, waiting for me to reciprocate, but I held my tongue. I thanked him for the meat and later, after it was dark and I was alone, I hung the shoulder up on the meat pole beside the moose.

The person I didn't see over the next week was the warden. I hung around the tent all day the fifteenth and sixteenth, even turning down an offer to go on another lion trail. But the warden and the biologist didn't show. Brian drove by to tell me he and Cary had treed a lion, a big female with three kittens, the kittens still in spots. They took pictures he said, and it was good training for the dogs, but they were getting a little anxious to find the big tom.

The next day Cary pulled up to the tent. He'd had some friends pull in for the weekend, to stay with him in his tent. "Drinkers," he said, grinning, "not hunters." He looked like a hangover was hard at his heels.

But, he went on to tell me, his friends had stopped at West Fork, to see if there was anything they could bring in, and they'd heard that the wardens had blown up a snow machine trying to get over the pass. "Fire. The works," Cary said, laughing, and for the first time I realized that in the eyes of the hunters the wardens were visitors, not people who stayed out here as they did, as I did, but just visitors. Slightly less competent visitors even. People who could cause trouble, but people who blew up machines trying to get over passes the hunters seemed to hop over like nothing. I thought of the way the wardens never stayed over, how they popped in and out in an hour or less, and I adopted the hunters' view. They weren't like us.

I asked if he knew when they'd be coming in again and he said that they'd loaded their burned-up machine and high-tailed it back to Idaho the same day.

Though I didn't like the idea of missing my January mail run I laughed with him about that, too. We were standing out in the snow, blowing cloudy breaths into the sky, laughing. We weren't in an office in Idaho. We weren't like that. We were the real thing. We were hunters.

13

Late the next morning Brian stopped by and said he was going up to Cary's, that they were going to hunt together today. He wondered if I was interested. Still wanting to see a mountain lion, I agreed to go along. Boone hopped peacefully onto the bed I made for her in the cab of the snow-covered pickup truck. She'd been in there a time or two, and seemed now to believe that I'd be back.

I crawled onto the snow machine behind Brian and we chugged upstream. His machine, he yelled back to me, wasn't really strong enough for two people, but once on the packed trail it ran fairly well.

At Magruder Crossing we rousted out Cary and Phil. Brian told Cary he thought he'd seen a track on the way over, the path of a lion crossing the river. We hadn't stopped and I hadn't seen anything, and I wondered what Brian was talking about.

Cary's friends were still in bed but Cary had his dogs loaded in no time; Phil took the back seat and they were off. Their big new machine was much more powerful and we struggled to keep up.

Only a few miles back toward Indian Creek the lead snow machine idled to a stop and we slid in behind it, our skis stopping just short of the peeling plywood dog box Cary towed. Cary stepped off his machine as if dismounting a horse. Brian pushed me back a little and I stumbled off so he could get up too. He met with Cary in front of the machines and I came up a moment later. Phil smiled at me as we all gathered around the lion track in the snow. He was wearing what looked like a second pair of Cary's wool clothing, things that didn't fit perfectly, and he looked at me while the others looked at the tracks. I was pretty sure he must be a client.

The snow was deep and light and the lion's path was nothing like the dainty paw prints of a cat on a driveway. I could see marks where the lion's chest scraped through the snow here and there, his legs punching deep holes. And even though the snow had fallen back into those leg holes, covering his footprints, I could still see the careful placement of each foot, each step in line with the last.

"Big tom," Brian said.

Cary nodded and looked up into the trees where the trail led. "Real big one," he said, glancing at Phil. He smiled widely. "This is the one you're after."

I kept looking at the track, the path of something big and heavy moving through deep, soft snow, and I wondered if there was any way to tell if the cougar was a male—a tom—or not. I didn't really think it was possible. It was probably one of the things the guides added to the show.

"Want to?" Cary asked.

Phil said, "Sure. If you think we should."

"Damn right I do," Cary said, still smiling. "He's not far. We got ourselves a hot trail."

Brian moved back to his dog box and slipped the pin. He kept the door nearly shut with his knee while he dug through the struggling pair of dogs, snapping leads onto collars. Then he let them push the door aside and he held the wiry, short-haired dogs back until Cary had his trio out too. They met at the lion trail and the dogs whined and barked, looking out of place here in the snow and dark firs. Mottled gray, black, and liver, they were what I always pictured as coon hounds, and I'd only ever imagined them baying through Southern swamps at night.

Since they had a trail this time they didn't keep the dogs on the leads, as they'd done when we'd chased the ravens. The hounds shivered as Cary and Brian tried to unsnap all the leads at the same time. It could have been from cold or excitement.

When the leads were off so were the dogs. They leapt wildly forward, dashing any which way, until the oldest bitch let out a bay and began to bound through the snow, directly in the lion's track. We stood without speaking for a minute or two. The dogs got farther away, barking and yipping now and then. I thought we should probably be doing something. Following them or something.

Then all the hounds began to bay and Cary said, "Locus has him strong," and both he and Brian went to their dog boxes and unstrapped the snowshoes from the top. They used the metal and plastic Sherpas, bragging about the teeth under the toes that held in the ice and hardpack. I strapped on my ash and rawhide shoes which were bigger and held me up better in the three feet of loose powder.

As we started into the trees, following the huge trail the dogs had mashed down, I kept wondering at the relaxed nature of our trailing. I asked Cary what would happen if the lion just ran. What if he took the dogs out forever?

"He'll tree," Cary said. "They're built for speed, not distance. Only once had one run. We didn't give up 'til it got dark. Had a helluva time getting back. Dogs started trickling in around three in the morning."

"That's when Beau got lost," Brian said. Beau was the prize pup he'd lost a few weeks earlier. He figured coyotes got him in the end and I pictured the tangle of tracks around the stain in the snow. "Lions won't mess with a dog," Brian said finally. "Less there's no choice."

Nobody talked for a while then. The trail was straight up a hillside that was nearly too steep to follow. We floundered along, sliding back and falling forward. It became impossible to hear the dogs over the pounding of our own breaths.

We crested a small flat and paused. The snow we'd stumbled through stuck to the wool we all wore and we began to blend into the trees. Phil breathed harder than the rest of us, and I guessed he wasn't used to the altitude. But he kept smiling whenever anyone looked at him.

The dogs' barking came back to us, still getting farther away. Cary guessed a mile and we left the trail and cut through clean snow toward the sound. I wouldn't have done that myself. I knew how sound could twist through the draws and ridges until it finally came from everywhere. Cary had done this for years, but I would have stuck to the trail, giving up the short cuts.

The next time we rested Cary held up his hand for quiet. No one was saying anything, but our breathing sawed through the chill air, wrapping us in clouds of vapor and sound. We held our breaths a moment and the howling of the dogs wasn't any farther. It was wilder though, angrier.

Brian nodded and let his breath out in a rush. "Treed," he said.

Cary grinned. "Big cat," he said. "Damned if he was gonna run far. Haul his big, lazy ass up a tree and take a nap."

He started off again, barrel-chested and pushing fifty, but excited now, nearly running, forgetting to give Phil time to get some air in his lungs. Phil unzipped the coat he was wearing, grinned and ran after him, sweat glistening on his reddened face. I brought up the rear, my big shoes wasted in the well-packed trail.

We raced through a small dip of a draw and lumbered up a south slope, losing speed in a hurry. The snow was still light, but deeper here, with only the scattered ponderosas sheltering the ground. I slowed down to keep from running over Phil, then slowed again. The slope kept getting steeper. Finally rocky teeth began to poke through, turning sections of the slope into cliff.

Cary stopped and wiped his face with a handkerchief. "We're getting close," he panted. "Hear 'em?"

Not too far up the draw I saw a thin, gray-blue line in the snow. I pointed it out, not able to tell if it was the dogs' track or just the old mark of something else, elk maybe. Cary laughed and said, "That's it. No wonder he treed early. Coming up this steep son of a bitch."

We waited for our breathing to quiet until we could all hear the unabated howling of the hounds. Cary shook his head proudly.

Circling around a jutting spur of stone, we found a narrow path between two sections of the growing cliff wall. We had to use our hands for the next stretch, swimming up the face more than anything else. At the top we rested again, our hands on our knees as we bent and tried to breathe slowly enough to get air in. Brian was the first one to straighten.

He clapped snow off his chest, lifting his shoulder holster to get inside his coats. He pulled out his binoculars and gazed along the sidehill to the next outcrop of rock. "Got 'em," he said.

We passed the binoculars around, all of us seeing the dogs leaping off the ground only to land back in the same place and bay and leap again. They were at the very end of the outcrop. A huge old ponderosa grew from the hill below, towering above the cliff by a good fifty feet. Ten feet of vacant space separated the dogs from the tree.

"We better get over there before they start jumping off the cliff," Cary said, and we started off again.

The walking was easier on our lungs now, but we were sidehilling from our outcrop to the hounds' and we had to lean into the hill to keep the trail from collapsing beneath us, sending us down the hill in our own avalanches. Our legs strained with the tension of trying not to slip.

When we reached the hounds they acted as if we weren't there. They were all shivering now, and it didn't have anything to do with the cold. They leapt to the brink of the drop-off, whining and howling, crazy about not being able to get at the lion. We edged around the lip of the cliff until we could see through the branches. The lion was a long, tawny rope of muscle lying quietly on a limb of the tree. It watched us through half-lidded eyes, as if bored and slightly inconvenienced, but not much concerned about waiting it out. The black tip of his tail twitched and he lowered his head onto his wide, soft-looking paw.

Cary whistled and said, "Boone and Crockett. Boone and Crockett easy."

Phil was still fighting for air but he smiled back at Cary and nodded. I didn't like asking questions that'd show my ignorance but when Brian came up next to me I asked quietly what Boone and Crockett was. He told me it was the name of the record book.

Brian took out his camera then and snapped several pictures of the lion and of the dogs. He tried to back up and get them into the same picture, but the branches blocked the view of the lion. I took a couple pictures myself, of the lion's face, his smoldering, gold eyes.

When Phil seemed to have his wind back, Cary and Brian began to wrestle the dogs again, snapping on leads and pulling them away from the edge of the drop-off. Even as they were hauled backward they kept leaping at the lion, flipping over and landing on their backs when the leads caught them short, choking and snarling. Brian sat down, bracing his feet against a rock, and Cary pulled a loop of the leads around a burned stump of a snag, holding the dogs with the tree. He looked at me and said, "If we'd let them, they'd follow him over the edge."

Then Cary told Phil they were ready. "Go ahead and take him," he said, and Phil almost seemed surprised. He stared at Cary a second, then reached beneath his coat, as if he'd just remembered his gun. From the black folds of wool he pulled a stainless-steel revolver, a .357 magnum, and looked at it in his hand. He'd taken off his mitten, and it must have been cold.

He walked to the spot where the view was best and he held up the gun. The cat wasn't twenty feet away and its expression didn't change a bit. Phil sighted along the four inches of barrel, then hesitated. He looked back at us, at Cary mostly. Cary smiled and said, "Into the chest. You don't want to mess up that head."

Phil nodded and turned back to his cat. I could see the gun waver a little and I wondered what was going on inside him. This had all been good until now.

The blast from the gun sounded small and ineffectual pointed into the vast spaces of the empty, snow-muffled draw. Even though I'd waited for it, the noise startled me a little, and I missed the very beginning of the lion's leap. By the time I was able to register what my eyes had recorded the lion was already in the air, not tumbling brokenly through the branches, but in full control, stretched wide from the power of his jump. I stepped to the edge of the cliff, standing beside Phil while Cary and Brian struggled to hold back the dogs.

The lion landed in the snow well below the outcrop, at least thirty feet below where he'd been lying on the tree branch. The same as jumping from the roof of a three-story building. I saw him just as he hit, disappearing in an explosion of soft snow. Before I could picture how broken he would be, he erupted from the snow in another leap that covered twenty feet, straight down the side of the hill we'd toiled up. His body began to ball up in mid-air and he crashed down into the snow again, only to reappear a moment later, stretched out and bounding. In a few seconds he was into the bottom of the draw and out of sight. No one had said a word.

Brian grunted, "Is he down?" His dogs had nearly pulled him over the rocks he'd used as a brace.

"No," I said, and Phil said, "I think I missed him."

"Missed him?"

"He's gone," I said. "All the way to the bottom and gone."

Cary wrapped his leash one more time around the old gray snag and tied it off. He walked up beside us on the rim of the drop-off and I pointed at the craters the lion had left in the snow.

"Well, I'll be a son of a bitch," he said. He laughed and clapped Phil on the arm. "Buck fever. Nothing to worry about." He laughed again. "Man, did he go." He shook his head and stepped back to his dogs. "You put the fear of God into that old boy, that's for sure."

He knelt down before his wild dogs and began to grab each one in turn, rubbing their heads and thumping their ribs in rough, friendly pats. I wouldn't have put my face or throat within their reach for anything. But it seemed to break the hold the lion had on them. Cary stood up and said, "Let's get them off this cliff and let them go. He won't be far."

After watching Cary, Brian did the same trick with his dogs. The hunters tugged their hounds back off the outcrop, out onto the trail we'd made through the steep sidehill between the sections of cliff. They knelt down and unleashed them again, and they were off down the hill, covering nearly as much ground as the lion had in his leaps, moving with a hint of the same supple grace.

They streaked to the bottom and were lost in the thick stuff, though we could hear them well in the cold air. "Won't be a minute," Cary said, and we stood on our snowshoes on the sidehill and waited.

Phil said, "I pulled up. Right when I pulled the trigger, I pulled up. I could feel it."

"You'll get another shot here in a minute," Cary said, and he held his hand up for silence. A moment later the shrieks of the hounds changed to that same maniacal yowling we'd heard before, when the lion had first treed.

"They've got him," Brian said, wrapping his dog lead around his waist. He started to slide down the path the dogs had made.

Phil and I glanced at Cary. He said, "That's that," grinning, and he whacked Phil on the shoulder again. "You'll bust him this time. Don't worry about it." He sounded like a coach trying to work a prized shortstop through an unexpected error.

Phil nodded and noticed he was still holding his gun. He slipped it into the holster beneath his coat and pulled his fat mitten back over his hand. His smile wasn't as steady or as strong as it had been before he'd pulled the trigger. Cary slid down behind Brian and Phil and I followed, all of us squatted over our shoes, ready to drop to our butts if we should start going too fast.

The lion hadn't gone a mile, and this time it was all downhill. We were on him quickly, without losing our breaths on the way.

The dogs had torn the area around the trunk of the tree almost to bare dirt. They'd prance and whine and howl, finally leaping against the tree, reaching as high as they could, bouncing off it back to the ground only to leap again. The snow around the tree was littered with the orange jigsaw-puzzle-shaped pieces of bark they'd knocked off the ponderosa's trunk. And I noticed the bright specks of blood scattered through the snow. At first I thought the lion must

Up top with Boone, fall

Last open water on the Selway

The Selway and Indian Ridge

Up top, early winter

Boone on the woodpile, early fall

Setting out, early fall

Lion hunter

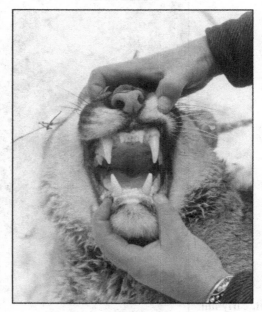

Teeth

Socked in. The thermometer box, horse ramp, tent, and truck are visible.

Channel work, spring

Inside the tent

Boone up on Indian Ridge,
late spring

have been hit. Then I saw that the dogs were biting the tree, cutting their lips, splitting their gums. The tree itself was ringed by a lighter band of fresh bark at the zenith of the dogs' bounds.

The lion was above us now, rather than at the eye-level the cliff had given us. Though he still lay stretched out along a stout branch, maybe fifteen feet over our heads, and his eyes were still only half open, he looked angry now. "Do they ever come out of the tree?" I asked. It felt less than safe walking around under him.

"Not while we're here. Not before they're dead," Brian said.

I took some more pictures. I walked around under the lion, even savoring the odd feeling of putting myself in such a position. He was tired now and his mouth was open a little as he breathed. I could just see a trace of the pink edge of his tongue. His eyes followed every move I made.

I put my camera down and Cary asked, "You done?"

I nodded my head and noticed that he and Brian both had their dogs held back, the leads stretched around the trunks of trees, well away from the tree the lion had chosen. Phil had walked up a small sidehill and sat down. From there he had a clear shot, no branches or needles blocking his view. I'd been mesmerized by the lion's heavy-lidded eyes and I hadn't noticed anything the men had done.

I moved away from the tree without looking back up at the lion. I sat down in the snow between Cary and Brian. It was as far away from Phil as I could get without putting myself on the other side of the tree, in his line of fire.

Phil had his gun out again and even in the dark timber I could see the sheen of sweat on his bare forehead. We'd been under this lion a long time, plenty long for any sweat from the hike to have dried or frozen. Cary's voice seemed loud when he said, "Let him have it."

Phil looked around the torn patch beneath the tree, then lifted his eyes to the lion. I watched him brace his elbows on his knees, wriggling them a little to make sure his stance was solid. Then he lowered his gun to a line between his eye and the lion. I saw him squint down the barrel, closing his left eye, and I saw how steady he went when he stopped breathing. Then I turned to watch the lion.

I'd stopped breathing when Phil had and I began to cringe as I looked at the lion, waiting for the sound of the shot, bracing for it. The lion was broadside to Phil and wasn't looking at him. He seemed not to be looking at anything now, just waiting for us to leave. Patient.

As I watched the lion's sleepy face I wondered when Phil would fire. And I wondered why. Cary and Brian had spent years training their dogs, Cary giving Brian the tips he'd learned himself. I could see their pride in the way the dogs worked, the way they treed the lion so fast, not once, but twice. Their pride was evident even in the way they cussed and tugged, holding back the barely tamed savagery of their hounds. I felt sure Cary was glad Phil had missed the first time. It gave him a chance to let his dogs out again. They didn't seem to be here just for the money, and I wondered why Phil was out here. What would he do with a lion skin back home in Philadelphia or wherever the hell he lived?

I kept waiting for the shot until finally I needed to take a breath. I looked away from the lion and the tree, hunching my shoulders in case the shot should come now that I was beginning not to expect it. I glanced at Phil just as he lowered his gun, and for an instant I hoped he'd realized what a letdown his shot would be after having seen the power unleashed in the lion's wild free-fall down the draw.

But in one big rush Phil let out the breath he'd held and laughed nervously. I saw him shake the tension out of his arms and rotate his head, getting the kinks out of his neck. Then he brought his elbows back to his knees and his eye back to his sights. He'd just held his breath too long, and now he was ready again. Maybe he hadn't thought about what he was doing at all. I couldn't tell. Maybe he had, but thought that this far into it it would be impossible to back down.

I had just turned to the lion when Phil shot. This time, in the heavy cover of the timber, the gun sounded sharp and heavy and lethal. The cat leapt again, straight up this time, over three feet, his mouth opened in a snarl or a roar that never quite made it out. His eyes went wide and his legs cartwheeled into a dead run, claws out, tearing at the branches he began to fall through, not completely unlike the spin of legs in cartoons.

As he fell past the branch he'd been lying on his right front paw caught it and he swung to a halt, hanging onto the branch with that one arm, the muscles thick and taut. He pendulumed there for a moment, graceful even in that. But his head began to droop, as if he was looking down, trying to select a place to land, and I saw the toes of his right paw begin to relax, the hard claws retracting back into their broad sheaths. The lion fell.

He struck one branch on the way down, spinning, so it was hard to tell if he was still alive or not. It was hard to look at his sleek, motion-filled body and imagine him being anything but very much alive.

I felt a little sick even before he hit the ground and suddenly I heard Cary erupt in a stream of swearing. I glanced quickly his way, wondering if he could possibly have felt the same sense of waste and loss. But he was cupping his hand under his armpit and his dogs were gone, having torn the leash through his hand fast enough to burn him. They met the lion at the same time it met the ground and Cary chased after them, still holding his wounded hand under his arm.

By the time he'd taken the five or six steps to the cat and dogs it was clear the lion had been dead before it hit the ground. Cary stood at the tails of his dogs, which worried viciously at the lion, tugging it this way and that, snarling through mouthfuls of fur and skin, ripping their heads crazily back and forth, the same way I'd seen dogs playing with blankets. I wondered what Cary would have done if the lion hadn't been dead.

When Brian saw the lion was dead he let his dogs loose, too, and they joined the melee on the dead cat. The hounds snarled and snapped at each other, only Cary's old bitch, Locus, never once relinquishing her stranglehold on the cat's throat.

I couldn't look away from the dogs. This had all been for the lion's skin. I said, "Won't they ruin it?"

Cary looked at me and said, "No. We'll pull them off before

they start to chew. This is their reward. It's good for them. Lets them get to know what they're after." I noticed he wasn't smiling now. Everything, for a moment or two, had turned serious. "Kind of spooky, isn't it?" he said.

When Cary and Brian began to pull their dogs back off, leaving Locus her hold until the last, I looked for Phil. He'd just stood up from where he'd shot; this time he remembered to put his gun away, hiding it quickly beneath his heavy, borrowed coat.

He walked slowly toward us, Cary and Brian and me, and the dogs and the lion. The dogs had calmed by then and the lion lay by himself in the trampled snow, his once smooth fur tangled and matted by the mouths of the dogs. We all stood over him for a moment and then Cary reached down and lifted a front leg. A small smudge of blood marred the white fur of the armpit. Cary said, "Right into the heart. Hell of a shot."

Phil smiled a little. "Now what?" he said.

"Tag it! It's yours." Cary started to laugh. It sounded like the first pull of a boat motor on a quiet lake. "The way you chased him back down we're almost back to the machines. Good plan."

He winked at Phil when Phil looked up. Phil's smile was gaining in strength. "It's big, isn't it?"

"Hell, yes. It'll make Boone and Crockett. Not tops, but up there." Cary knelt down and pulled back the lips of the lion. "Look at those choppers."

The canines were ivory white and over an inch and a half long. They looked healthy. Cary said, "That's a record book head."

Phil's smile kept gaining confidence, and I saw how he was putting the letdown behind him. He was already starting to rearrange this so it would be something he could tell about later, something he could even think about with pride and satisfaction. I said, "Do you remember how it jumped?"

Cary glanced at me and Phil looked down. Cary said, "Like it was stung by a bee. I knew you had him as soon as he jumped like that."

"No," I said. "I mean out of the first tree. And down the draw.

I've never seen anything like that in my life."

Cary looked at me again, not smiling. Brian bent down and hauled the cat up from the snow. It was as long as he was. He draped it over his shoulders and said, "Might as well start." The dogs followed after him, almost like pets now.

Phil walked by me, without meeting my eyes, moving after Brian and the dogs. Cary followed down the trail the others had beaten into the snow, and as he passed he clapped me on the shoulder. Like a coach helping me past my error.

I stood in the quiet trees, looking at the trampled snow—the broken orange bark and flecks of blood the only bright spots in the white and gray of the woods. A moment later one of the dogs yelped and I looked up, almost startled to find myself alone. I hurried down the slope after them.

14

After carrying the lion to the road we stood and posed as a group, the lion at the center—the guest of honor. The river, as always, commanded the background. When we all had our pictures Brian decided to run back to Magruder Crossing with the others instead of returning to Paradise. They asked me to come with them for the celebration and then asked again. I didn't feel a lot like celebrating this, but I climbed onto the back of the snow machine, part of the group.

Cary's friends were sitting up in the tent by the time we got there, the fire stoked, sipping beers and laughing. They came out into the snow and admired the lion and I watched Phil's face redden, not with embarrassment, but with pride. Cary talked up the whole hunt, mentioning the spring out of the first tree, but skimming over what had caused it, the missed shot.

He set to work skinning the cat, peeling the skin clear down to the toes, so the rug would have claws. He moved his knife so quickly and carelessly I was sure he'd slice huge holes in it, but he finished without a nick. He left the head on the hide, saying he'd let the taxidermist earn a little of his money. I laughed at that and looked around, but I was the only one out studying this. Dusk was closing in and the rest were in the tent already. They'd been talking about a feast since we'd pulled up.

The naked lion carcass, hanging upside down from a hind leg looked smaller but even more powerful than it had with its blurring coat of fur. Each muscle group was distinct now, sheened by a silvering outer sheath of tissue. It did not however, look graceful, or like anything that had ever seemed so much alive. All that had been left on the mountain, and I did not pity it, or feel bad any longer. I was interested in how the skinning was done, how the skull would be removed, what would be done with the carcass. I tested Cary with a few questions and soon he was a fountain of information.

When I asked about the meat he grinned and dove his knife into the body, behind the shoulder, along the spine. "Butterflies," he said. "Big, beautiful, butterflies."

He sliced the loins away from each side of the spine and handed one to me. The meat was whitish pink, more like pork than anything else. We carried them into the tent and a whistle went up from the men in there. Cary sat down with a flourish and began to butterfly the loin chops. He cut a steak nearly an inch thick, but stopped before he'd cut all the way through. Moving his knife over an inch, he cut again, this time finishing the cut. He pulled the meat away from the rest of the loin and let the center cut fall open. The two wings of the butterfly spread and the chop doubled in size. I marveled at the simplicity of the trick, already planning to repeat it with my next moose steak.

As they cooked a huge meal of fried potatoes and canned vegetables, dropping the chops into a sizzling grill at the very last, the tent filled with the mix of smells and the whiskey bottles got lower and lower. I remembered the times like this in the fall and I remembered why I craved those nights in strangers' tents. But these men no longer seemed like strangers, and I laughed at their stories about long-running lions and mutton-headed dogs, laughed until I thought I might suffocate.

The dinner was delicious, but nothing could have touched laughing like that. I hadn't out-and-out howled with laughter since I'd been in here. I'd come to enjoy living here, but it was a peaceful thing, contented, rather than anything like a belly-buster. I wiped tears from my eyes, as did the others, and like the others I took more and more on my plate until the pans were empty, and refilled my glass when the bottle was passed.

When the dinner was over and the party was done Brian stood up and said he had to get back to Paradise to take care of his dogs. I had to leave too, for Boone, locked all day in my truck. Cary's friends would be leaving in the morning and I said my goodbyes. Then Brian and I moved out into the night on his snow machine.

He had a flashlight taped to the cowling for a headlight but the night was crystal clear and before we'd gone a mile the moon broke over the ridges, round as an eyeball. Brian pointed it out, as if that were necessary, and I broke into a last tired giggle. He turned off the flashlight to save the batteries and we rode on, following the river, washed in moonlight, the snapping cold of the bright air stinging my face and any other trace of skin it could find. After months of walking it seemed nearly miraculous that it was possible to skim along so smoothly and so quickly. The whiskey was still running lightly through me and, racing through the clean, cold, silver world, I felt like tipping my head back in howling laughter at the moon.

Brian dropped me off at the channel and raced on alone. While I chopped at the new ice I thought of the miles of river he would see and I wished there were some way to keep skimming along like that. I shuffled through the snow to my meadow and threw open the truck door. Boone bounded out, leaping into me as she had after her night in the fifty-gallon drum, only able to see me as her rescuer, not her imprisoner.

The tent would be stone cold after a day away and Boone was tugging at my heavy deer-hide mitten, her signal for play. I tossed her around and soon we were into a full-fledged rumble, tearing up the meadow, soaking ourselves as we rolled and twisted in the snow. Finally Boone lay victorious on my chest as I panted beneath her, snow shoved beneath my collars, the moon still bright above me, already on its way down to the other side of my narrow sky.

≈

I continued to see the lion hunters for the next week or so, even

bumping into Brian once as he was pulling a bobcat out of the mountains near Paradise. He'd trailed it alone, with just his dogs and his
smile nearly split his face. He'd shot it in the tree, he said, killing
it, but it hadn't fallen down. He told me about using nearly all his
bullets to shoot the branch out from under the dead cat, and how it
had simply fallen to the next branch and hung up there. Finally he'd
had to climb the tree, and he had the scratches to prove it. The
cat was a big one though, he told me, and would bring hundreds of
dollars, enough to pay for all his expenses for the weeks of hunting.
He never stopped smiling.

But by the twenty-seventh of January the lion hunters all pulled
out. They said they might or might not be back, they couldn't be
sure. The day before I'd walked down to Paradise to give the rangers
a call, to see if they knew anything about when the wardens might
be coming in. The ranger I talked to said, as far as he knew, that after
blowing up their machine they weren't due in until the middle of
February. It seemed as if, for the first time in a long time, I would
have some time to myself.

And, though I wouldn't have believed it in October or November, I was truly looking forward to that. I was tiring of the daily whine
of snow machines, of the constant possibility of company. I realized I
hadn't really done any hiking, except behind dogs, since I looked for
my dad and brother. I'd fallen into a trap of waiting around my tent,
just in case somebody should come by, somebody who might invite
me to some sort of social activity.

I'd also been waiting for privacy for another reason. The temperatures had been nearly perfect lately, mid-twenties during the
day, only dipping a few degrees below zero at night. But I hadn't
been able to put the fear of that first near thaw behind me. The more
I thought about it the more I realized how hard it would be to accept
the waste of all that moose meat.

I did not mind killing, but not to waste. After trapping the
raccoon I'd delved into my *Foxfire* books for a recipe and I'd roasted
the coon whole. I'd even gone out on a limb and mentioned my fear

of waste to the lion hunters before they left. On their last day in Cary brought down the remainder of Phil's lion carcass, the meat untouched since the loins had been removed. I think he meant it as a bit of a joke, but I hung it up in plain sight, and cut steaks off it now and then.

So, soon after I heard Brian's snow machine fade to a whisper up-river, the last of the lion hunters to leave, I moved up Indian Creek to the meat pole and trudged back with a front quarter of the moose —the leg and shoulder assembly. I made another trip for the other front quarter and I leaned them up against my table, beside the stove, where I could let them thaw. Tomorrow I was going to slice them into pieces as big as my forearm, just like the book said, ideal for preserving. That afternoon I mixed up the curing solution—salt and pepper and most of the few other spices I had. Once the meat was cured it'd be set for any thaw that might come along.

I wasn't sure if all my secrecy about the moose was bordering on paranoia or not. The fine for poaching would probably equal a month or two's wages, but that was the least of it. I couldn't imagine what the wardens would think of one of their own employees breaking the laws. I didn't know if they'd have special rules for that or not. And there was always the threat of Old Ironsides, the warden who'd bust his mother. I wasn't even sure if he was real. The one thing I did know was that I'd rather not find out, and in the back of my mind I wondered if I wasn't simply making a game out of all my precautions. Something to do.

As evening rolled around I left the quarters to thaw and took my pipe out for my usual stroll, staying out of the tent as long as possible before the long winter night forced me inside for another fourteen hours. I was nearly to Raven Creek, two miles up the Selway, when I stopped to listen to a plane. There were often jetliners slicing over above me, and occasionally something military would rip over, leaving heart-stopping sonic booms in its wake. But this sounded like a small plane, flying low, and I stopped, surprised by the sound.

It was a moment more before I realized I was not listening to a

plane, but to a snow machine, still a long way off, the sound rising
and falling depending on the river's twists. I wondered which hunter
had forgotten something, marveling at the idea of their incredible
mobility. Already I was nearly an hour from my tent. Who knows,
they could have been all the way to Darby before they realized they
had to turn around.

As the machines grew louder I had a slight queasy feeling about
the moose legs in my tent, but the hunters never went in there and
I started to smile before the machines were quite around the corner.

Then suddenly before me were two Idaho Fish and Game snow
machines. They roared up and shut off their engines and as they took
off their helmets I recognized the biologist, but not the warden. The
biologist introduced me and I heard the name of the one warden I'd
been warned about—Old Ironsides. He was real. I pictured the huge
white and red quarters propped against my table, unavoidable, unde-
niable evidence of the crime of feeding myself, and my bowels grew
loose and my throat went so dry I picked up some snow to suck on.

The warden started asking questions immediately. When I'd
called to Paradise the day before, the forest ranger had asked about
the lion hunters and I told him they'd all be heading out today. This
warden had screamed over from Idaho to catch them before they
got out of the mountains. He'd caught them at the top of the pass.
I imagined Cary and Brian being as shocked as I was. I wondered if
they'd done anything wrong—if they felt as hopelessly caught as I did
right now.

Along with his bobcat, Brian had shot a lion a few days before
and the warden wanted to know who had really killed them, which
client had filled out the guide's tags. I told him I'd seen him come out
alone with the cat, and I was sure the lion was his too.

He asked about Phil next. Cary didn't have an outfitting permit,
he said, and he was sure as sure that Phil was a client. I was pretty
sure about that myself, but I told him Phil was a friend of Cary's from
Hamilton, that he was unemployed, so how could he possibly afford
to pay for a lion hunt? That's what Cary had told me once, and at the

time I thought it had been an odd thing to say. I'd wondered why he bothered telling me anything about it. Now I wondered if I'd been included as much as I thought I'd been, or had I been a wonderful opportunity for alibis?

The warden eyed me suspiciously, not at all pleased with my answers, but I figured he had me red-handed and I might as well go down in flames all by myself. I wondered if he'd make me ride all the way out of here wearing handcuffs. They'd said he'd tack my hide to a tree.

The biologist broke up the interrogation, stepping around the warden to pet Boone. He said it was getting nearly dark and if I'd hop on the back of his machine they'd give me a lift back to Indian Creek. They were going to spend the night at Magruder, he said.

My mind raced, stumbling onto a thin possibility. "You guys don't need to give me a ride. I don't mind walking." I gave them a great smile and added that I did a lot of walking.

But they insisted and my hopes sank until I thought about Boone. "What about Boone?" I said. "She can't ride."

"We aren't that far," the warden said. "It can chase along behind."

Now I thought I might have a real chance. "With all the hunters snowmobiling by, Boone's started chasing the machines like crazy," I said. "I've been beating on her, trying to get her to quit. I can't let her chase us now."

The warden nodded, seeing the sense of that, and the biologist dug under the cowling of his machine. He brought out my mail, including a round metal candy tin painted with holly and other Christmas stuff. He grinned, shaking his head. "This was with me when my machine blew up," he said.

Half the paint was scorched away. "It was wrapped, but all that kind of burned up."

Giddy over what appeared to be an unbelievable escape, I was glad to have an excuse to laugh. I opened the tin and held it out to the men from Idaho so they could see the solid block of chocolate filling one side of the tin, bits of the crinkly red paper that had once surrounded the individual candies poking through here and there. We all laughed out loud and the warden said, "Meltdown!" and we laughed harder. He wasn't such a bad guy.

The biologist also handed over a huge T-bone he'd bought with his own money, and I almost felt bad taking it from him. He said he wasn't a giant meat eater, but that he thought he'd get to miss it after a while. At my tent I had half a moose, a quarter of a deer, and most of a lion, but I made a big show of my appreciation, and when he finally handed over a bag full of oranges I really was bowled over. I'd missed nothing as much as fresh stuff, fruit in particular.

I thanked them both profusely and as they were strapping on their helmets the biologist said that he thought he had his wife nearly talked into coming in to trade with me for a weekend. He said he thought he'd be back with my boss in a couple of days and he'd let me know for sure then. I told them to come on down in the morning for coffee, but they said no, with everyone gone there really wasn't anything for them to do and that they'd be out first thing.

They turned their machines around then and drove off upstream, toward Magruder, away from everything incriminating I'd left in my tent, and I stood still until I couldn't hear them any longer.

Then I turned back toward my tent and though it was nearly dark I walked slowly, unable to believe how close a walk I'd taken with disaster. When I reached my tent I pulled the quarters out to my food cache and I buried them in there for the night, just in case the warden would roar back with some piece of conveniently forgotten mail.

I spent that night in my usual rush through the mail and then I sat back in the candlelight and opened the fire-blackened tin of candies and stared at the solid mass of chocolate, the red, crinkly papers frozen into the block. I picked at the chocolate with my knife and popped a piece in my mouth. My grandmother had sent it in and she would have died if she'd seen what had happened to it. But I hadn't had a sweet in months and though I was constantly picking little bits of soggy paper from the tip of my tongue and the chocolate tasted a little like smoke, it seemed pretty deluxe. I tipped back in my chair and laughed, imagining my grandma being able to picture any of this.

I waited until after noon the next day, but I never saw that warden again. I retrieved the quarters and spent the rest of the day hacking them into forearm-sized chunks and rolling them around in the salt. I was supposed to hang them after that, someplace dry, and I still hadn't figured where I would do that. Late that night however, lying in bed, I thought of the horse tack building down at Paradise. There wouldn't be a horse in here until June. I smiled, thinking about curing my contraband right in a Forest Service building.

By the next morning the meat was soggy, the salt drawing water out of it as if from a sponge. I wanted to leave it hanging until it was dry, but I'd finally learned that people had a bad habit of popping up at the worst times and I dumped the meat in a garbage bag and loaded my pack to the brim. I had to sit down beside it, using my legs to lift, and when I had it up on my shoulders I wondered that my legs didn't simply bow until they snapped.

The pack weighed over a hundred pounds and I thought about splitting the meat into two trips, but I was started now, and I wanted to get this stuff out of my tent.

I tottered the first few steps of the six miles to Paradise, then plunged through the well-packed snow machine trail. The extra weight was too much. I was caught off guard and I went all the way down, the pack impossible to control once off balance. I managed to fall backward though, and lying on the snow, looking at my leg still stuck in the trail, I knew that if I'd gone forward or to the side I would have blown my knee to shreds. I slipped out of the pack straps and went to the tent for my snowshoes. This was going to be a long day, but it was early still, and as I staggered up under the pack again, I thought of the Scott party in Antarctica. This was nothing compared to that.

I was nearly to Paradise and nearly exhausted when I heard the whine of a snow machine coming up behind me. I glanced quickly around, but there wasn't even a tree to hide behind. I let myself fall against the bank, swearing, knowing this meat was going to be my undoing, but too tired to care. In a minute the Paradise outfitter pulled up beside me.

We talked for a minute. He was just coming in to make sure his camp was closed up tight. There was a chance he'd be back in a few weeks with one more hunter, but he wasn't positive. I stood up as we talked and he kept looking behind me, finally asking what I was doing. I told him I was just moving some stuff down to the ranger station at Paradise.

"What stuff?"

"Odds and ends, you know."

He nodded and said, "Looks heavy."

I said it was but declined his offer for a ride. I was almost there, I told him.

After he drove off I stepped back down onto the snow machine trail, only then noticing the reddish brown stain in the snow where I'd rested. I reached back and felt my pack. The bottom was soaked, my hand coming away slick with the meat juice the salt was drawing out. There were already a few red drops in the trail beneath me. I pictured the red drops leading all the way back to my tent, like Hansel and Gretel's crumbs.

I looked up at the sky, wishing I'd just buried the damn meat, but I trudged on, wondering if the outfitter would be there to watch me hang it, wondering if he'd ask if I needed a hand.

But the outfitter's camp was another half mile beyond the Forest Service buildings at Paradise and I did not see him again. I had to dig the snow away from the tack room door with a snowshoe, but once inside the meat hung perfectly. Before I was done the room smelled of pepper and muddy red drops were beginning to stain the floor. I wondered how I could stop that, eventually deciding it wouldn't matter. Let them try to figure it out in the summer.

Instead of sticking around and chancing another run in with the outfitter, whose curiosity could only have grown, I strapped on my empty pack and started the hike back to Indian Creek. It was a long march but, at the beginning anyway, relieved of the crushing weight of the soggy meat, I felt as if I could nearly fly.

It was dusk when I reached the salmon channel and found two empty snow machines parked on the road. They weren't Fish and Game and I followed the tracks down to my fish. Inspecting the waterfall at the end of the frozen-over channel were two snow-suited men. Their faces were still red with the cold and I knew they hadn't been here long.

They introduced themselves and wanted to know all about what I was doing here. They let me know that they'd been in my tent, looking for me. They kept talking about how impressed they were that I'd actually spend an entire winter in here alone. It was the kind of talk I'd reveled in during the fall, but now all I could think was that these sons of bitches had just walked right into my tent, poked around in my home without an invitation, without a thought.

I asked if they were lion hunters, I asked what they were doing in here, just stopping myself before asking what *the hell* they were doing in here. They weren't lion hunters, they said, but simply Sunday drivers. "Get out of Hamilton for a day," they explained.

I nodded, as if I could understand that, and mentioned that it was getting late, nearly dark, and that they'd better be getting to wherever they were planning on spending the night. They laughed at that as we trudged up the hill to the road and their machines. They were spending the night in Hamilton, they said. Back at their houses, in bed. They said they thought my tent looked pretty nice, but sure not nice enough to spend a night in. They zippered up their black nylon snowsuits and waved goodbye. Their headlights cut a path before them as they zoomed the last forty miles of their Sunday drive.

I walked slowly back to my tent, picturing the places they were passing. Raven Creek, Magruder Crossing, Magruder itself, then up Deep Creek toward the pass, scooting by the phone at Hell's Half Acre, then the lonely sheds at Slow Gulch and the broken old cabin of Blondie's.

In the dark, with their headlights closing off the world beyond the brightness, they would not be able to see any of that, but I could.

Easily. And, as I put a few more pieces of wood in my stove, shivering from cold and exhaustion while I waited for the heat to take hold, I realized that most of my anger at those nonchalant Sunday drivers was fueled by envy. It was just so obvious that they were doing whatever they wanted.

When the stove began to glow red I took off a few of my wool shirts and started fixing dinner. I decided on a mixed grill—deer, moose, and lion—knowing sometimes a good meal, just working on one, could pick me up.

As I butterflied my first moose steak I whispered, "Picked a hell of a weekend to cure that meat in privacy," trying to make myself smile. I gave a tired chuckle, but it only reminded me of the aching ribs I'd had laughing with the lion hunters.

After dinner, sitting back in the murky lantern light, waiting for my tea to steep, I heard the sudden rumble of yet another snow machine. It came from downriver, Paradise, and I knew it had to be the outfitter. I sat without moving as I listened to it cross the bridge over Indian Creek and shoot through my meadow without slowing or turning, late now to be crossing the pass back to the rest of the world.

I remembered how the lion hunters had laughed at the wardens for being visitors. But the lion hunters were all gone now, too, and I was the only one who was still here, alone. I reached for my tea and for my book, but I thought of the warden's questions and I wondered again if I'd only been used as an alibi by the lion hunters with whom I'd laughed so hard.

I didn't have much of a heart for reading then and I carried my tea outside; as I stared up at the frozen stars I sipped at it, feeling its steam condense against my cheeks in the black night air. I was not just a visitor.

15

With everyone finally really gone I began to hike again. There was no one to miss if I wasn't at my tent—no hunters zipping by on their snow machines—so I was out nearly every day. I spent a lot of time up high, enjoying the long-distance views and the long hours of sun after being hemmed into the tight canyon for so long. For quite a while the weather held clear . . . cold at night, but beautiful during the day. Even though it was in the twenties I'd often hike with only a shirt on, my coats tied around my waist.

I hoarded the oranges the biologist had given me, taking one a day and saving it for up top. Picking an open spot, a rock or the base of some huge old ponderosa, I'd have lunch—cold meat leftovers from dinner, saving the orange for dessert. Just the smell of the orange could take me to places far from this frozen world. When I was done I'd suck on snow. With the flavor of the orange still bright in my mouth I could almost pretend I was a kid again, doing my paper route, sucking on a popsicle.

On the first of February the biologist returned, this time with my boss, not Old Ironsides. There was little reason for the visit, but it had been scheduled after the aborted January trip, so they came on in. The mail had been brought a few days before, so there was not even that. We walked around the channel as usual and the warden said everything still looked very good.

They stayed their normal half hour and just before leaving the biologist told me to hike down to Magruder sometime around the twelfth, to let them know who to call in Missoula to come and pick me up. He grinned, saying if everything worked out he was coming in with his wife on the fourteenth—Valentine's Day. He'd snow machine in and I'd snow machine out. Three days later we'd trade back. A long weekend he called it. My vacation.

They left around two, as the Selway's steep walls blocked the sun for another day. After hearing about my vacation I couldn't sit still, and I grabbed my snowshoes and raced up Indian Ridge until I was back in the sun again. From up top I could look over the endless series of snow-covered, wind-swept ridges that surrounded me, leading in the east clear out to Montana, to the Bitterroot Valley, running straight to Missoula. I could barely believe that in two weeks I'd be riding up that valley in the Deerslayer with Rader, a visitor on the outside.

Eventually the weather broke, the skies growing overcast, spattering snow. I kept walking all day, even when the temperature began to climb and the snow, often as not, became mixed with rain. The mountains, while a little less comfortable, were just as impressive in the moodier weather. The clouds shredded on the ridge backs, torn fragments hanging on in every draw. The snow fell from the trees in great thumping clots, making walking in the woods a little spooky. And, without the trees' bright mantle of snow, the world turned a dark, dark green, nearly black, with the gray shards of clouds hanging everywhere, the white of the snow still clinging to the ground. A black and white world. When I walked high enough I would be inside the clouds themselves, distance turning to gray nothingness, the rain beading directly onto my sodden clothes in tiny crystal spheres.

Then real snow returned—with wind—thick, wet, heavy stuff that clung to every needle. The world was once again white and I walked through all of it, returning to my tent in the evenings caked with the same soggy wind-driven layers as the trees.

Up high in the draws of Indian Creek and Sheep Creek I found giant snowslides. They were avalanches really, but I called them snowslides, which sounded less dangerous—less like something that could bury me without a trace. Then I found one on the Selway, a few miles down toward Paradise. It had crushed across the road, half covering the channel of the river itself. Walking home from that I was startled by a sudden whispering rush that grew instantly to a crashing roar. I whirled in time to see a huge cedar come splintering over across the river, crushed down by the great weight of the snow.

That evening I stood outside my tent, looking up through a blizzard at what I could see of the mountains. In glimpses between the waves of cloud the trunks of the trees, plastered with sticky snow, stood out starkly white. I studied the width of my meadow, trying to picture the thundering walls of snow, wondering how much of the open they could cross. I went back into my tent and stood beside the stove, my soggy clothes steaming, and I thought the avalanches would probably peter out before they reached my thin canvas walls.

Eventually the dismal weather, despite its beauty, began to wear on me. The constant dampness and the soaking wool got old. I began to spend half days in my tent, fiddling with projects, making moccasins, repairing ripped wool, oiling rifles, reading, cooking. I was working through the back sections of the moose and the cuts were so good I could hardly believe it. I had whole dinners of nothing but meat and tea. I gorged.

The closer the fourteenth drew the more I dwelt on my trip out to the world. I packed a box of things I would take with me, gifts mostly, like the ones I'd made for my family at Christmas. I also packed a rump roast the size of a three-pound coffee can. We'd have us a feast out there. Finally I'd have a chance to share at least one tiny part of my world.

On the tenth I started out for Magruder, to have the West Fork boys give Rader a call. It was a Saturday and I guessed they could catch him in our dorm room and ring me right back, letting me know he really would be waiting out there for me on the fourteenth. I could already picture that—the Deerslayer parked at the great wall of snow at the end of the plowed road, Rader leaning against the hood as I rounded the last corner of a forty-mile snow machine drive, my first ever.

The lion hunters had returned a day or two earlier, but I hadn't seen much of them. I'd kept hiking, no longer feeling a need to be at my tent should they happen to call, not quite able to put away my suspicions that they'd used me as a tool in their game with the wardens. I only made it as far as Raven Creek when I bumped into Cary, and we stood in the road and chatted. There were more snowslides across the road and he bitched that they blocked his trails. He said the snow had sunk down so much, and had gotten so stiff and dense, he guessed lions might nearly be able to walk over the top of it. He hadn't cut a track in two days.

As we talked Boone's ears pricked up, and a moment later I heard more snow machines heading our way. A big train rounded the corner and I recognized the Paradise outfitter on the lead machine, followed by Brian and a couple more guys I didn't know. The place seemed to be getting crowded.

As his machine stopped Brian stood up in the saddle and waved, pointing his mittened hand back at the other machines. I squinted against the whitish haze in the air and one of the guys stepped off his machine and threw his arms into the air. "Fucking Fromm!" he shouted.

Though for a moment more I couldn't believe it and I stood stock still, it was true. Rader. And Sponz. My mouth dropped open and I started running as fast as I could in my snowshoes, plowing past the hunters. I caught Rader in the stomach with my shoulder and we rolled rumbling off the road, into the deep stuff covering the brush beside the river.

We got up spluttering and then I jumped Sponz. I could feel the eyes of the hunters on us and I knew this wasn't a mountain man picture, that we must look like children playing beside their snow fort. I didn't care.

But later, when the hunters moved on and Rader and Sponz chased after them, riding tandem on their rented machine and leaving me to walk the two miles alone, I couldn't help looking at things through the eyes of the hunters. Rader and Sponz had left Missoula the day before with plans to get here yesterday, but they'd blown a belt on the way up to the pass and had spent the first night up there. On Saturday they'd been limping their machine back toward Montana, giving up, before the hunters came along with a spare belt, and the knowledge of how to use it.

Then they'd roared back on in, leaving the hunters and their heavily loaded machines far behind. It wasn't until they'd turned onto the Selway that they hit the snowslide. Rader took it at full speed, Sponz hanging on for dear life. But as the machine tipped on the slide's steep side, Sponz baled off. Rader had stayed with it, tumbling all the way down to the river.

Somehow he wasn't hurt, but the machine's windshield was smashed, the fiberglass cowling cracked. And it was stuck. They'd sat there for an hour, sweating and swearing, wondering what to do. Then the Paradise outfitter had come along again, and together they'd been able to manhandle the machine back onto the road. Ever since then—even now—Rader had followed them like a shadow.

Walking along the empty road I pictured how the hunters had smiled and shaken their heads as Rader and Sponz told their story of one amateurish screw up after another. We'd all stood about in the road, laughing, and I'd wished that the hunters would just go away.

I thought of the expressions the hunters and the wardens had worn when I told the story of my father and brother's aborted ski trip. They couldn't imagine a more foolhardy plan. Why hadn't they just rented snow machines? Part of the truth was that they wanted to ski, but I knew the other part, the part I never mentioned. Snow machines had never occurred to them. We'd never seen one before, never considered using one ourselves.

But I put all their doubts out of my mind and hustled the last mile downriver; Rader and Sponz and I crammed ourselves into my tent that night. I laughed through the storytelling until I couldn't stand it any longer, laughed even harder than I had with the lion hunters.

We spent the next day poking around in the woods, looking for grouse, mooching around. The temperature hit thirty-seven and the new snow began to thump down out of the trees again. One falling clump hit me in the head, firing down my neck like a frozen bullet. Though that wasn't the first time that had ever happened, it was the first time it was funny. Occasionally we'd hear the roar of snowslides, glancing around toward the sound of the louder ones as if we could see the rushing walls of snow through the heavy cover of the trees.

The next morning we started out early and headed for Magruder. I wanted to show them the cabin there, my ideal home. The road was covered with slides ranging from small, pure white trickles that just reached the road, to huge, muddy, boulder-strewn barriers that blocked the road and the river, bright peeled logs poking out like broken teeth. It was hard just walking over them and we wondered how we'd ever get a snow machine across.

We stopped at Cary's camp at Magruder Crossing, but no one was in and after stopping to throw snowballs at the first open spot I'd seen in the river, we trudged on to Magruder. The slides we crossed now had a path cut over them, a thin flat spot the width of a snow machine over the wild pitch of the slides.

Halfway to Magruder we ran into Cary, digging tiredly at yet another slide blocking the road. He swore and swore, sweat covering his face. He said he'd been shoveling for two days straight, and he was halfway to Magruder—two miles. Most of the work he'd done the first day was covered over again that night. Rader and Sponz really began to wonder how they were going to get out.

Cary began to make a plan for us. At Magruder we'd get shovels and begin to dig back toward him. He was sure Brian and the Paradise crew were digging up from downriver, and once the four of us met up we'd begin digging back toward them. "Til we can all get the hell out of here," he said, but in my head I thought, Not quite all.

Cary also asked me to use the phone at Magruder, to have them call a bunch of his friends to start digging in from that side, to call his wife and let her know he'd be out when he could. Rader and Sponz said they'd need to call their girlfriends too. Leaving Cary to his digging, we pushed on.

I put the call through to Montana as soon as we reached Magruder. They said they'd make the appropriate calls and, just before I hung up, I told them they might as well call the biologist in Idaho too. "It's hopeless," I told them to let him know. There was no way he and his wife were going to get in or out, and he might as well stay home.

I didn't feel very good canceling all my hopes that way, but soon we were cooking the gigantic rump roast I'd packed to take out with me. It came out beautifully and Rader and Sponz didn't stop talking about how great it was.

That night Rader and I stayed up late, talking, or chewing the fat, as he called it. He was thinking of getting married, he told me. Soon. To Lorrie. At first I was sure it was a joke, and I wanted to wake Sponz up for confirmation, but he was serious. He wanted me to come out for the wedding and I wondered how he figured that would happen. He started laying plans and then, in some wild leap of logic, he began planning how I could come out now too, as soon as we got the road cleared, how I could ride out with one of the lion hunters.

I went along with him, knowing full well it wouldn't work. The hunters would definitely be pulling out for good now, and they'd be dragging everything their machines could handle. There wouldn't be room for me.

In bed that night, listening to the quiet snoring around me, I could not believe Rader was getting married. The last time I'd seen him and Lorrie they hadn't even had a date. That had only been four months ago, but now it seemed much longer—forever. I began to wonder what else was going on out there. How much was I missing?

≈

The next day I wormed through the snow-blocked doors of the tool shed and retrieved three shovels. The digging began. We worked like slaves, the crusted boulders of packed snow nearly as hard as ice. We detoured around the rocks and tree trunks embedded in the snow and the trail snaked around the smaller slides and over the biggest, some twenty feet or deeper. By nightfall we all had blistered hands and we hadn't yet reached Cary.

The next day we got up wearily, trudged back down our old trail, and began digging again. We saw a few slides fly down the hillsides, small ones, once having to sprint up the road to avoid being overrun.

By mid-afternoon we met Cary and dug our shovels into the snow and leaned against them. The big group of guys at Paradise had already reached Magruder Crossing. We had a trail clear to Magruder, and the way the road and the mountains lay from there on out to the pass it looked as if they could make it out the next day. The Paradise guys had already headed back to close up their camp, and would be making the push out first thing in the morning.

Rader and Sponz decided they'd hike down to Indian Creek, to their rented machine, and begin packing up their stuff. They'd spend the night there, then attach themselves to the Paradise train in the morning. I'd hike to Magruder and clean up our mess and pack up all the stuff they'd left there. I'd either spend the night there alone or hike back here and spend it in Cary's camp.

I wasn't crazy about wasting the last of the visit that way, but Rader didn't want to have to detour into Magruder to load up his stuff the next morning. As wild as the hunters seemed to get out while the getting was good, Rader doubted they'd wait for him to finish screwing around. They'd had so much trouble getting in when the road was still open, Rader sure didn't want to have to try getting out on his own, not when there were other people to stick to if he could.

When Cary, the expert, the lion hunter, said it sounded like the best plan, it was sealed. I hiked up alone to Magruder, Boone tagging at my heels. Once the cabin was cleaned and packed I couldn't stay. Without the endless talking of Rader and Sponz the old cabin was emptier than ever. I hoisted Rader's pack onto my shoulder and though it was getting late I started back to Cary's camp.

I reached Magruder Crossing a few minutes before dusk, and a few minutes after that Cary and I heard snow machines. Three of his friends roared up, their machines bristling with axes and shovels and picks. The rescue party. They'd dug through a few small slides but said they'd waited until they figured we were through the worst of it. Within half an hour four more rescuers showed up.

It was a crowded night, with nine of us in one tent, and we stayed up late again, telling more stories and lies. Though it could have been as much fun as any other time like that, my head was down at Indian Creek, where Rader and Sponz sat by themselves in my tent, likely as not starting to get a few butterflies about inching their machine through the hairpin curves of our narrow, crumbly trail, trying above all else to stay up with the experts. Safety-in-numbers kind of thinking.

I was going through my own butterflies, even packed into the laughter inside the crowded, smoky tent. Everybody really was out of here for good now, and after the long days seeing my friends I was afraid the river and the mountains and the trees would no longer be what they had come to seem. I thought they might once again crush down with the November loneliness. I imagined the last exhaust fumes, the last roar of machines taking everyone away, and my long walk back to my tent through the drizzle, over the shaky trails, already grown useless, that we'd dug with such a sense of urgency. All more safety-in-numbers thinking.

In the morning one of the rescue machines headed downriver with a handful of spare belts for the Paradise crew and I hopped on for the ride. But we met the whole gang of them not far away. They must have left Paradise in the dark. Rader and Sponz were already in their shadow position at the back of the pack and Sponz started to tell stories of going over the slides sitting behind Rader, his life flashing before his eyes. He wondered why in the world we hadn't made the trails wider.

But the outfitter yelled back that it was time to move. "Get the hell outta here before the whole goddamn mountains slide down," he said. There was nothing left but to shake hands with Rader and Sponz and wish them luck. They wished me the same and roared off. I started off then too, alone in the drizzle, just as I had pictured. When I reached the tent I stoked up the fire and read the last note they'd left for me and I could feel the blues roaring in at me with as much power as the biggest of the avalanches.

I jumped up and checked the channel, cleaning out the slightest scraps of ice, though with the warm weather there wasn't nearly enough to block the flow. With that done I started to bring in water, and firewood. I swept the old carpet viciously, not leaving the slightest wood splinter stuck in the nap.

Then I crushed the empty beer cans, working feverishly just for the sake of busyness. I swept away every trace of the visit, hoping it could return to exactly how it had been before. But already I was hearing their laughter, and the reek of their cigarettes still clung to the canvas. I'd never once before guessed that could be a smell it was possible to enjoy.

My plan worked well until nightfall. Though I didn't have much of a heart for eating I forced myself through the motions, then sat at my table wondering what to do next. I remembered that my trade with the biologist had caved in at the last moment and I wondered if I'd ever get out of here. I thought of the outfitter yelling about leaving before the mountains themselves closed off any escape, and I felt that I alone had been too slow.

I glanced around the gloomy tent and, as usual, when my gaze swept over Boone her tail thumped a few times. I swallowed back the dryness in my throat and reached for my big deerskin mitten. I put it on and shook my hand, slapping the mitten back and forth, the signal for play. Boone was up in a heartbeat, her teeth locked onto the leather, and I began shaking as hard as I could. Her growling grew more frenzied but she would not be shaken off.

Soon we were in the meadow, where the rain had turned back

into snow, and we scurried after each other in the darkness, me shouting and Boone barking, the heavy, sodden trees soaking up all trace of our voices.

It wasn't until we were heading back to the tent, soaking wet and panting, that I remembered that it had been Rader, Rader and Lorrie, who had thought to go to the pound to get Boone for me. Now they were getting married. And I had missed the whole thing sitting in here, playing mountain man.

16

I tried to get back into the swing of things during the next week, tried to recall my days of hiking, the feeling of relief when the lion hunters had first left, the way I'd enjoyed finally being alone again. But I couldn't get over how the biologist's plan had fallen through, how Rader's visit had degenerated to little more than frantic snow shoveling.

Before a week had passed I began to plan a march out. I could reach the outside in two days, I figured, nighting over at Blondie's. Once on the road I'd keep hiking until I could pick up a ride, at least to a phone booth where I could give Rader a call. The way the temperatures had been I knew the channel could get along fine without me. I felt I'd been cheated out of my vacation and I wasn't going to let that happen. I was going to get back to the world. I was going to have my long weekend.

As soon as I decided to leave the sky cleared and the nights got cold and I worried about the channel. But the water had warmed to above freezing and ice no longer clogged the exit the way it had during the cold snaps. After checking several mornings in a row I decided it would be all right. It began to snow that night and I was able to pick up the Boise radio station. The weather report sounded perfect—no new cold wave threatening—and I loaded my pack carefully, taking a few of the presents I'd give out once in Missoula, but that no longer seemed so important. Just getting out was the main thing.

I woke early the next morning and the sky was full of stars, not clouds. I ran quickly down to the channel and made sure it was all right. Then I threw on my pack and started the march for the pass. Beneath the new stuff, the snow was crusted with the cold, hard enough to support my weight, until nearly noon anyway, when the sun would warm it and I'd begin to plunge through again. I carried my snowshoes on my pack and the walking went fast. Blondie's was twenty-four miles and though I knew that was a long haul, I didn't think it would be much trouble. I pictured the look on Rader's face when I showed up at his door, pack on my back, wool everywhere, sheepskin mukluks on my feet, Boone at my heel. My hair was long enough now that I wore it tied back in a ponytail. I'd be like some kind of apparition.

I left before dawn but the sliver of moon and the stars gave me more than enough light. I moved quietly through the night's layer of soft new snow, silvered and shadowed. It was nice to be silent again, after the weeks of every crunching step on the frozen snow. I went up and down over the slides and two miles had slipped quickly by before Boone's hackles suddenly went up. She stopped and waited for me.

I was leaving for civilization and, for practically the first time, I wasn't carrying a gun. I moved slowly forward with Boone. The only other time I had seen her hackles up was the frigid night she woke me with her growling and I'd flipped the flashlight on in time to see a cow elk pull her head from the front flap of my tent.

We rounded a bend in the river and came to just another empty dirty snowslide. The dawn was just starting to give enough light to see. I looked at Boone, but she was still hanging tight to me. As we started up the slide Boone began to growl. I slowed, but I was curious now.

At the top of the slide I found a dead mule deer doe. Its flank was split open and steam rose from the wound. I remembered Boone's growl and I glanced around the shadowed trees surrounding me. I poked around but could find no other injury. There were no footprints either. Uphill from where the deer lay I could see a dent in the snow, and then another one a little farther down, with a slide mark to the body from that. Like a hit, a bounce, and a slide.

I looked at the cliff above me. It would have been a free-fall of forty or fifty feet. But deer don't just fall off cliffs. I looked around again, but could find no more clues. Boone had stopped growling when she found the deer. She sniffed at it and sat down.

Circling around again, I came up with a drag mark. This was going away from the deer, down the slide. It was easier to see on the softer snow. It was a smooth depression a few inches deep, maybe eight inches wide.

I checked the deer one more time, rolling it over. It was very fresh, the insides still hot. I could think of no reason for a drag mark other than some animal dragging off a piece of the deer. But there was nothing missing. Had there been two deer? I checked again and didn't think so. There wasn't any blood in the drag mark either. None of this made sense and I glanced again at the dark trees before I started to follow the drag mark.

I turned the first bend and the drag went straight ahead through the fresh, flat snow, around the next bend. There were no footprints anywhere, just this smooth dent in the snow. I had no idea what I was dealing with. Boone started to act funny again, hackles up, growling, and I really wished I had a gun.

I moved ahead on tiptoes, walking beside the track, thinking I would probably have to come back over all this to study it again, and I didn't want to walk over the clues.

We rounded the next bend and Boone charged. The drag mark led straight to a bobcat sitting in the road. By the time I saw it, it had spun around and was taking a swipe at Boone with a bare-clawed front paw.

Boone reversed her charge a hair short of those claws and came back to my side. The bobcat glared at us, then turned back around and started dragging itself down the road. It veered toward the cliff side, making for a snow hollow under a tree.

I was putting two and two together by now. The bobcat and the deer had gone off the cliff together. The deer had been killed and the bobcat crippled. It was obviously paralyzed from about midspine down. I watched it crawl up toward the tree, where its back would be covered and it could make a last stand. But the uphill was tougher going and it had to stop and rest. It had already dragged itself two hundred yards from the deer.

I watched a moment more, too surprised to do anything. The drag was left by its left hip and leg. Black spotting edged the flank, where it switched from the mottled tan and buff of the back to the clear white of the belly. The bottoms of the useless feet where black, with black hair between the toes. Dragging its hind quarters like that had covered the tracks left by the front paws.

Going up the slight rise to the tree, it could only take three or four steps before stopping to rest. Its mouth was open, panting, and I could see a pink edge of tongue. It must have been equally broken up inside.

I thought of the bobcat Brian had killed, of the vast amounts of money the pelts could bring in, but more than that I saw the heaving of the bobcat's sides as it struggled for every breath, the obvious pain of picking itself up to drag itself along another few feet.

I picked up a large rock from the edge of the river and carried it cocked back in my right hand, ready to come down on the crippled cat's head, wanting to get this over with as quickly as I could. I remembered the raccoon I'd caught in the trap by the channel. That seemed like years ago now, but I wanted to finish this cat just as quickly.

The cat heard my approach and glanced over its shoulder. Then it turned around. To face me. It hissed, like a house cat, but louder and meaner. It made a flashing sweep with a front paw, claws out. Then it started to drag itself toward me, its eyes flashing, yellow, malevolent squints. Even mortally injured, it was coming at me, something that towered over it, outweighed it five to one.

Its eyes never wavered and it was hard to pull mine away from them. But it kept coming for me, waving its claws, hissing, spitting.

Pretty soon I took a step backward. Boone growled and the cat really hissed then. It lurched two steps forward, its ears laid back on its head, almost growling itself, like a smaller mountain lion roar.

I dropped my rock and retreated to the river edge. I kicked around until I found a limb of a dead cottonwood about eight feet long and stout, thicker than a baseball bat, but I wouldn't have minded if it was longer. I came back up the bank and the cat was sitting still, collecting itself.

When it saw me, its ears went flat again and it started toward me. I lifted my club and stared into those yellow slits of eyes. I had never seen anything so angry or determined.

I tensed just before swinging the club and the cat stopped. It seemed to know what was coming. Its head dipped toward its shoulders and I brought the club down as hard as I could possibly swing anything.

It broke across its head and the cat was dead. I swung once more, to make sure, driving the cat's head and shoulders deep into the crusted snow, glad anyway that the swing was clean and fast.

I stared at the cat for more than a minute, studying its sides for any trace of a breath. Then, leaving the cat there, I circled around the cliffs, climbing to the top. I picked up the deer's tracks at the edge of the cliff and followed them backward, amazed at the wild turns and twists the trail made. There were no cat tracks though. Then I found a clump of deer hair. Then another. The cat had been riding the deer through all this, tearing at her.

That went on for about eighty feet. Then I saw the divot in the snow that was the cat's last bound before landing on the deer. There were only two divots, leading to a snow pocket beneath a small pine, where he had lain in wait for the deer. The deer had passed within ten feet of the tree, its tracks showing that it was walking slowly, browsing.

The first bound mark of the cat was only a few feet from the deer tracks. Then the deer had leapt and the cat was after it. There was the final bound and then the mad, twisting, turning dash off the cliff. I looked over the edge at the dead deer and bobcat. I wondered if the deer had seen it coming or if the cat snapping and clawing on its back had driven it beyond that.

I crawled carefully back down the cliff and picked up the cat. It was surprisingly heavy, probably pushing forty pounds, and I let it back down and sat in the snow beside it. I petted its fur smooth, never having imagined such a death. But I began to picture my triumphant arrival at Rader's dorm room again, only now the picture was enhanced by this giant bobcat draped casually across the top of my pack. It'd be a bitch hauling him out all that way, but I strapped him on my pack, unable to resist the idea of that picture. How much more mountain-manly was it possible to get?

I hiked quickly, all those pretty pictures dancing in my head. The road was covered with new, trailless slides that slowed me down, but I made Magruder Crossing in two hours, good time for six miles considering the delay of the cat. My legs were feeling the extra weight of the pack but I crushed on, wanting to get to Blondie's before dark. I came up the next slide, spooking a cow elk that had bedded down right in our shoveled-out trail on a snow slide. Her eyes bugged and she was off, crashing cross-river and disappearing into the trees. I called Boone off and kept plodding.

By the time I reached Magruder the adrenaline rush of finding the cat had worn off. Even the pictures of my amazing mountain man self had begun to tarnish. I knew I had to call out to West Fork, just to make sure no one was coming in, and I dropped my pack off on the road. Then I crashed down beside it. The extra weight was really doing a number on my legs and I sat in the snow, rubbing at them. After a few minutes rest I picked my pack up again and hid it beneath a tree. Then I shuffled off to the cabin and its phone.

Before I called I came up with a plan to get Rader down to the trail head, cutting out any walking or hitchhiking once I was out. I would ask the rangers to call him, telling him that a friend of mine was coming into Missoula at four the next day, and asking Rader if he could give him a ride down to the trail head. I would use the name of

Rader's best friend back in Ohio, a person I had never met, and hope Rader would get the idea. I was smiling when I picked up the phone and cranked the handle. Ingenious.

When the ranger answered I asked first if they knew when the wardens would come in, my usual reason for calling. He didn't and he ran off to check, leaving me to rehearse my plan one more time. This was going to go off smooth as silk. I nearly giggled. Then the ranger got back on and said the wardens were due in in a week. I made quick calculations, wondering if my snowshoe tracks, in and out, would still be obvious by then. It'd be cutting it awfully fine.

Then the ranger said that in the next day or two a bunch of Forest Service brass was going to be touring in on some sort of fact-finding mission. He said the place should be crawling with biologists and bureaucrat types. Before he got a chance to ask if there was anything I needed, anything they could bring in for me, my plans had crumbled and vanished. I was beginning to feel cursed. Would I never leave this place?

I said no, there was nothing I needed. Then I thought a second and said, "Maybe some candles." I liked their light. I made a last ditch effort, saying the slides had gotten even worse than they'd been, new ones blocking the road all over the place. He said thanks, and said he'd pass the word on to the brass. He said it'd do them good to get off their asses a little for some real work. I laughed like I should and we hung up.

I stood for a moment staring at the phone and I started shouting swear words at it. Son of a bitch! Not only had my great hike out turned into yet another pipe dream, now I couldn't even stay here tonight. The brass would undoubtedly use the cabin.

I stomped back up road to my pack and threw it onto my shoulders, already having forgotten exactly how heavy it really was. I groaned and started back down my own trail. I was going to walk twenty miles today anyway, in one big circle.

Going the other way killed my spirits nearly as much as turning my back on my father and brother had. Halfway back to Indian Creek

I could hardly put one leg in front of the other. I'd stop every mile and rest, usually just dropping the pack and falling beside it in the snow. But I began to realize how hard it was to get the pack back on, and I started to fall over with it still on. When I peed during one of my breaks, without bothering to stand up, I knew I was getting bad. I stripped off my pack and walked to the river for a drink. I fished my cup into one of the little holes that'd been opening in the river ice and sat and drank. Then I crawled back to my pack and pulled the cookies Rader and Sponz had brought in. They were rich, home-made, chocolaty, nutty, coconut-topped things that stunned me with their incredible flavor. I hadn't had anything like that since I'd been in. I ate the whole bag as I sat and watched my legs tremble.

I was at the old ford the Nez Perce Indians had used to cross the Selway on their journeys from their Idaho home to the buffalo hunt-ing in Montana. On their trail it was still possible to see nearly girdled old trees. The Indians had stripped the bark off to eat, noth-ing else available in the hard country of the mountains. I thought I could picture their desperation to get through this country and out to the promised land of Montana.

I put on my pack and hiked deeper into the mountains, to my tent. When I passed the mule deer the bobcat had killed a flock of ravens scattered noisily and a lone immature bald eagle flapped off the carcass and flew heavily, silently downstream. I followed after it.

Back home I threw off my pack as if it had attacked me. I stoked the stove and crashed back on my bed, thinking of carrying that cat eighteen miles, when I'd found it two miles from my tent. I tried to be mad at myself, but I started to laugh out loud. And I thought Rader and Sponz had looked like greenhorns. I wasn't ever going to get out of here, and I began to realize if I'd gone a day earlier or later I would have missed the whole bobcat story. The whole time I was worried about what I'd miss outside, in civilization, I'd never once wondered what I'd miss in here.

I sat up and slid my slipper moccasins onto my feet. I was nearly glad I hadn't made it out. I'd have my whole life in civilization, and only a few more months in here.

After dinner I pulled the bobcat from my pack and set to work skinning it. I remembered every move Cary had made skinning the lion, and I followed them as if they were law. As the skin came off huge areas of blood-shocked meat were exposed, giant bruises over the left hip and the center of the spine. The spine was broken, as was the hip and the leg. I wondered if the cat had been caught under the deer when it hit. It certainly hadn't landed on its feet.

I checked the teeth. The canines were split and broken, not from the fall, but from age. There was not one that was intact. They were about one quarter their healthy length and dull and flat rather than sharp. That desperate charge hadn't had a chance with no teeth to finish the deer.

I'd never really guessed that things like this happened and I realized again that it was simply luck that I'd been able to find out about it. If I'd been in town yucking it up with my friends I wouldn't have seen anything at all.

I finished the skinning, making one tiny hole in the belly I fretted over terribly. It was late now and I was beat. I rolled the skin carefully and set it in the cab of my truck, the one place safe from everything, even mice.

I stayed close to my tent for the next several days, waiting for the invasion of the Forest Service brass. I visited the dead deer, wondering when the coyotes would find it, wondering if I could see the eagle again. Where had it come from? How had it known there was meat available? As I kept waiting for the Forest Service curiosity and boredom drove me to the kill again and again.

I discovered that the ravens set out guard birds, one upstream and one downstream of the carcass. If I walked down the trail I would see a raven launch from a tree several hundred yards before I got to the kill. Then I would hear it cawing and by the time I was within sight of the kill there would be nothing there but raven tracks. The eagle was still working the carcass, but it would flee with the ravens. Its tracks stood out clearly in the chaos of the raven prints, as long as my hand. I could barely believe how big the eagle really was.

I began to play a game with the ravens, sneaking around through the trees trying to take them by surprise. They always caught me if I followed the river, which had become a highway for everything since it'd iced over. I tried circling wide, going up on top of the cliff and peeking my head over the edge. I had them, fifteen ravens working on the deer. I laughed and they erupted, quick black shadows flitting through the trees, fleeing danger. They never did figure out the high approach and I'd often catch them working on the deer, or, if the eagle was on the carcass, they would be standing all around, ready to move in as soon as the eagle left.

Four days passed before the coyotes finally hit the carcass. Their tracks pounded the area flat. There was a little splotch of greenery left from the deer stomach and a pinkish stain in the snow. Same as ever.

I followed their tracks into the kill, six of them coming in from across the river. They dragged the deer all over the place and it was hard to follow. But I saw the scuffs around the one hole in the river ice, the water running black three feet below the snow and ice covering it. At the downstream edge of the hole I could just make out an inch of leg and the deer's split toes, six inches under water. The ice hid everything else and I wondered if they'd lost the whole deer or if I was only seeing a broken scrap of leg.

I grinned again, imagining the frenzied tearing, the yanking this way and that and the sudden slip and splash, six coyote faces staring down into the black water, suddenly quiet. I let my face go all stupefied, imitating the coyotes I pictured, and I said, "Oops."

I laughed out loud. That was the last trace of the bobcat and the deer, the eagle and the ravens. If I'd left I would have missed it all.

17

The Forest Service crew never did show up. I wasn't terribly surprised. After going through the work of digging out, something that had to be done to escape, I doubted that a bunch of office workers would do that same kind of work just to mess around in the mountains for a day or two.

I stayed close to my tent though, just in case, and a few miles upstream I discovered an otter den—two holes in the snow across the river, long slide marks connecting the holes to the water. Crushing through the soggy snow, I made a den for myself beneath the sweeping black branches of a spruce, and I waited to spy on the otters. Boone huddled with me in this cave, her coat matted with rain. But the branches kept off most of the drizzle and I staked out the otters for two full days, glad for something to do.

On the third day the first otter popped out of an opening in the ice a hundred yards or so downstream. Once on the snow it ran several steps and launched itself onto its belly, slithering across the snow, pushing with its back feet when it began to lose momentum. Then it would pop up into a run and leap again. As soon as it reached another opening in the ice it disappeared into the water. It was up at the next hole, sliding across the snow until it found another spot to enter the river. I grinned, wondering how it could find its way in that fast, black water.

Eventually I saw the whole family, four of them, and I went back up to the den day after day to watch them play. One came up with a fish—what looked like a sucker—and sat beside the hole in the ice and ate it whole, chewing on it from the head down, like a cold, bony hot dog. The busy crunching came loudly across the snow and ice.

Nights were long, cold interruptions keeping me from the play of the otters, but the socked-in weather did hold in radio waves and I spent an hour every night listening to the radio, as much as my battery supply would allow. In one of those hours I learned that in little less than a week Idaho would be right in the path of a full solar eclipse.

I spent a couple of days watching the sun and the clock, picking a spot to watch from, and found that at the scheduled time the sun was neatly framed in the notch between the ridges of Indian Creek. I chose a rocky pinnacle that would get me above the trees and hoped the weather would cooperate.

I was out right after breakfast on the twenty-sixth—eclipse day— but when I climbed up Indian Creek I found that the snow was still crusted hard and I couldn't climb the pinnacle. I stood staring up at the snow-covered point, running my hand over its glossy burnish of ice. Without the pinnacle's height I could only hope to catch glimpses of the sun through the trees, what suddenly seemed like the only view I'd had of anything for months.

I took out my knife and poked at the layer of ice, chipping off bright, brittle shards. Soon I cut a complete foothold and tested it, pushing my foot in and lifting my weight. It held and I cut another, and then another. I cut and climbed until I was at the top.

At the peak there was just enough room for me to sit cross-legged. Boone, stuck below, whimpered for a second or two, then curled up in the snow on the side of the ridge, glaring at me.

The sky was a solid, seemingly hopeless overcast, but I tried to believe that it seemed thinner in the east. Then suddenly the notch really did begin to brighten and I saw the edge of the bright ball of the sun in the haze. It rose quickly, and for a few minutes it seemed as if one side was darker than the other. I waited and nothing changed.

I looked at the wind-up clock I had carried with me. Could that have been it? That dull dimming? I glanced around my gray world and felt pretty foolish for cutting my way up here for that, glad nobody was here to see this.

I waited a little longer, staring at the bright gray east. The wind-up clock was less than accurate and I usually set it by guess anyway. Maybe something was still supposed to happen.

By now the sun had burned through to form a clearly defined disk at the top of the notch in the mountains, the haze thick enough I could look at it without being dazzled. Then, too suddenly to be believed, there was a piece missing from its southern edge. I double checked and there was no doubt. This was not a new thickness of clouds, a light dimming on one side or the other. An actual slice was being taken from the side of the sun.

I looked away. The radio had warned and warned about being blinded by watching the eclipse. The world got darker slowly—slowly enough that it was hard to notice. I glanced back and half the sun was gone.

The mountains were darker now. I looked down at my camp and the Selway. It looked like evening, the time of day I would usually be about here, getting back to camp before dark.

Now there was just a sliver of sun edging the left side of the dark ball that had replaced it. That was the moon, I knew, but knowing that didn't mean anything. I stood straight up on my tiny pinnacle and watched as the last of the sun winked out.

Where the sun had been there was only a hazy, fluctuating ring of brightness. That's all. Around me the woods were truly dark. The snow on the open slopes in front of me glowed pure blue, more definite than at any twilight, as if there were some force under there that wouldn't be held back forever. The chickadees were silent for once. It seemed to get a little cooler but I don't think that was possible. Boone whined and then it was completely quiet.

The vague ring of light wavered above the notch in the mountains, the sky blue-purple from horizon to horizon. The green-treed slopes across the creek faded to murky black.

I circled on my pedestal, my fists clenched and my skin tingling. It was truly dark, the snow still glowing blue, nearly pulsing. In the southwest the second dawn of the day began. A first tentative paling grew ruddy red, the color of the darkest wild rose. This spread across the sky but the intensity died, as if there were only so much color to give.

I looked back to the sun as the moon edged aside and day broke again. The snow returned to its normal white, the blue retreating beneath the surface where it was just barely visible. The sun returned to its full orb and there was no longer any trace of the moon. A bird chirped and, tentatively, others followed.

But still I circled, tingling on my little perch, trying to see what was no longer there, what I had not had enough time to see in those too full few minutes—trying to take in all that I had looked over for months, as if the second dawn had shed light on more than just mountains.

I shouted. I raised my fists above my head and shouted. As I continued my demented circling on that spire, I knew that everywhere I could see, and far beyond that, on everything the sun had just transformed, the only footprint on the land that wasn't some animal's was mine. I shouted again, big enough to burst.

Whooping, I slid off the pinnacle and Boone charged in. We wrestled around on the crusty snow and then we just flat out ran, as if there was nothing in the world that could ever stop us.

Later that day it rained and I tried to stay busy in my tent, but I couldn't keep away from the pinnacle. By late afternoon I slithered back up, my toeholds grown slushy, and I stood on top, watching the notch and the rest of the world around me. I tried to squint, hoping the blurring would make it easier to picture again the morning's transformation. But that light was gone forever. It was not something that could be captured, even in the mind. Already I was questioning the blueness of the snow, the redness of the sky. But, even though I couldn't see it, I smiled, knowing it had been there, that I had seen what no one else had.

Then, as the day's real dusk closed down on the Selway, I slid back down and strolled to my meat pole. There was only a steak or two left and I meant to cut them down and finish them off in one last feeding frenzy to celebrate the eclipse. But when I reached the pole I found that something had beaten me to the feast. The last bit of spine hung from its rope, the only meat left clinging in thin, frazzled strands. I found the tracks of the marten, saw how it'd climbed one tree and inched along the meat pole, sliding down the rope and gorging itself before dropping straight from the meat to the ground. The drop forced his footprints into the hard snow beneath the bones. I remembered that in the fall, during my trapping initiation, I'd mistaken squirrel tracks for marten. "Be the world's biggest squirrel," I said, shaking my head and cutting down the last trace of the moose and pitching it into the trees. The marten could finish it now without acrobatics.

The next day I hiked down to Paradise and picked up my cured meat. It was much lighter with the water drained away and I was glad of that. Walking back, I whittled slivers off a chunk but I'd gone pretty heavy on the spices and the meat was a little hard to handle. I guessed I'd be making a lot of chili, using the hot meat and the pounds and pounds of beans I still hadn't figured out any real use for. I had three months left here and I wondered just how sick of chili I'd get.

It kept drizzling off and on for the first week of March, the temperature creeping up the thermometer a little higher every day. Finally I stepped out of my tent one morning to find that the sky had cleared. The temperature that day reached forty-four, the highest point since November.

The snow was really beginning to melt and I spent the morning digging it out from around my tent. All winter long I'd used the snow as insulation, but now it was seeping through the canvas and my tent was thick with the smell of wet cloth.

The old snow was hard and stiff and I had to cut blocks to pick up and throw aside. Before I was done I'd stripped off even my union suit top, hardly able to believe how the sun felt full on my back. I smiled, watching my naked arms bulge as I lifted the blocks of snow and felt the coarse, hard crystals melt against my chest. It seemed I could feel everything.

The next day was as clear as the last and when I poked out into the clear blue I took off immediately, even skipping breakfast, my snowshoes strapped across my back for later in the day, when the night's crust would melt off. I hiked all day, stripping off shirts one by one, eventually even unbuttoning the top of my union suit, the air against my skin a wonderful sensation.

From the very top of the mountains I studied the peaks around me, picking out drainages I knew, and though to the east Trapper Peak stood out alone, gleaming white on the edge of the Bitterroot Valley, it no longer drew my eye the way it had before. I turned back to the world I knew, picking out the drainage of the Little Clear-water, hiking south and west until I could see the Selway's path, far below, swinging through a long bend. I knew that curve was the Nez Perce ford, and I grinned, almost surprised by how well I'd learned this country, how I could know it from any angle.

I slid down the mountain, the snow this high taking on a strange, hard slickness. The top inch or two turned soggy in the sun, full of big, wet, slippery crystals. But, beneath that, the frozen crust was still rock hard. Occasionally I'd slip and go all the way down, sliding through the soaking slush without making a dent in the crust, without being able to punch through for any kind of handhold. I'd have to slide until I reached a rock or a tree I could grab on to. Though I never picked up great speed, the slips spooked me, my imagination pitching me off cliffs where, dreamlike, I could tumble forever before crushing back to the black spruce and granite-like stretches of snow.

As I got lower, coming down from the mountains that afternoon, the crust gave away and I had to put on my snowshoes. Shuffling along, I ate the last of the little blocks of Wisconsin cheese my aunt had sent in for Christmas, things like Edam and Brick and Gouda that I didn't remember having eaten before, when I lived in Wisconsin.

Cheese wasn't something I'd brought in and the new flavors were something I'd tried to dole out to myself, to savor. In the wild, warm sunlight I threw my hoarding to the winds.

I was switchbacking down the last steep southwest slope above the old Nez Perce ford when, at the base of a towering, red-barked, ponderosa pine, I stumbled across open dirt. I just stared at it for a moment. It was the first ground I'd seen in four months.

I chugged across the hill and sat down in the two foot circular patch. The dirt was actually thawed, muddy, covered with pine needles. I dug my fingers into it and laughed. It smelled like mud and wetness, with the hot scent of the dead needles. Some of those things I hadn't quite realized had smells.

Boone rushed over when she saw me on the ground and soon we were rolling in the mud and the snow. I threw snowballs at her that she caught without slowing her mad charges into my chest.

As I picked myself up a sudden whistling, whirring rush filled my ears, and I ducked instinctively, as if someone had launched some kind of missile. I glanced up in time to see a pileated woodpecker streak by, wings tucked firmly to its sides, screaming through the air. It flared above the trees below me and disappeared in the branches. I'd never seen one fly that way before, and once I recovered from the noise of its rush I wondered if the return of the sun was turning everything a little wild.

I remembered the eclipse, and though I knew it was not an event connected with weather, I couldn't help associating it with the changes taking place. The blue glow of the snow in the momentary darkness seemed to foretell the changes I saw now, as if the energy beneath the ice was finally emerging. I couldn't keep away from it, and I spent the following day up top, too.

This time I went north, chasing herds of mule deer from draw to draw, bumping into an occasional elk or two. I decided to stretch my walk to Sheep Creek, thinking I might be able to see some bighorns, the animal whose picture had drawn me out to Montana in the first place.

The crust acted different today, slushing over the same as ever but occasionally giving away beneath me even way up high. Breaking through unexpectedly was unpleasant, like miscounting the number of stairs, jarring my hip and knee that way, and I strapped on my snow-shoes and kept on, worried more about the effect of the coarse, wet snow on the rawhide webbing than I was about the lack of traction the snowshoes gave on the sidehills. On the really steep sidehills I'd take the snowshoes off, kicking in steps with my boots, leaning uphill.

I pushed on for Sheep Creek but the ridges began dropping away in cliffs I couldn't get around and I kept looping farther to the east, until I was worrying about how far away from home I was get-ting. I worked my way into a corner and I started to hurry a little, not bothering to take off my shoes for the next steep pitch.

My feet went out from under me so fast I hit the ground before I knew I was falling. I built up a head of steam in an instant. I tried to dig my knees and elbows into the snow but the crust was hard here and I only scratched away the surface slush. There was a cliff below me someplace and I thought I was going too fast to ever stop when suddenly my knees grated over rock and I grabbed with everything I had, ripping open my fingertips. I came to a stop, breathing so hard I wasn't sure if I'd ever get another breath.

I waited a minute, making sure I was really there, then reached to my belt for my knife and cut myself a knee hole. With my knee wedged in I cut a handhold. I kept going, as I had up the pinnacle to watch the eclipse, but this time I was trembling, and I concentrated on not looking away from the rough surface of the snow immediately in front of me.

I didn't stop cutting holes for myself until I reached a tree I was able to straddle. With a leg safely around each side of the trunk I peered down my path. The track of my slide—the bright crust wiped clear of slush—went right over the edge of the cliff. I closed my eyes and rested my face against the bark of the tree. My feet must have been dan-gling in space. My heart began to race, as after a close call in a car, when the driver's had a moment to think of what has just nearly happened.

I stayed there several minutes, wrapped tightly around that tree, before I reached out to unhook my snowshoes. With the snowshoes looped across my back I circled around the way I'd come until I found the first chance to drop down the side of the mountain, leaving the land of the cliffs behind.

Clouds were closing off the sky before I reached my tent that evening and I never did see a sheep that day. And I never did get over how close I'd come to wiping myself out.

The rains resumed during the night and for several days I was content to lie around my tent again, cooking and reading, listening to the steady patter on the canvas. I read all of *Atlas Shrugged*, a gift from my sister, and followed it up with *Tales of the French Foreign Legion*, a book my dad had included to lighten up the Graham Greene and Franz Kafka he'd sent in the same box. As the rain mumbled on and on I marched through the baking desert with the legionnaires.

I was just attacking a Muslim-held outpost in the sand when I heard a pair of snow machines whine upstream and abruptly turn silent. I snapped the book shut and grabbed my coat and headed out. In a few moments I saw the warden and a Forest Service ranger walking into my meadow. They'd been running around the new slides, out onto the river ice, threading through the trees on the opposite bank wherever the slides had run clear across the river. But when they reached the last one, just a little way above my meadow, they said the ice looked too rotten, and they'd decided to hoof it in from there.

They carried an armload of mail and apples and oranges, even some eggs and bacon. After the standard channel inspection they stayed long enough to have some sardines and crackers for lunch, the three of us cramped in the small, smoky tent. They were gone within an hour, and, as usual, I was tearing into my mail before I heard the last of their snow machines.

All the mail was great, but the highlight of the whole stack was a rare letter from my little brother, Joe. A senior in high school, he'd been swimming for four years and his letter told of his trip to the state finals. State! I couldn't believe it. The state meet had been nothing but a dream for any of us when I'd been swimming. He'd clipped an article from the school paper, including a photo of him with his head shaved. State and a shaved head! My punky little brother! I just couldn't believe it.

I whooped, startling Boone, but when she saw how excited I was she dove in and we wrestled around like pups. I'd send her flying, shouting, "Can you believe it, Boone? Joe shaved his head! Joe made it all the way to state!" When she'd land Boone would already be turning back to me and we rumbled for nearly an hour. Then I went and read my mail all over again. I read Joe's letter and his article three times, whispering, "Way to go, Joe!"

But that night, for the first time since my first or second mail run, my high was followed by a swooping low. Joe comes out of nowhere to set school records, to go to state. For all I knew Rader was already married to a girl I hadn't even known he was dating. Again it seemed as if everything was slipping away without my having a chance to join in on any of it. That fast I could go from thinking I was living the world's greatest life to feeling I was trapped in here forever.

To take my mind away I dove into a new book that night, *Papillon*. The story of a man condemned to Devil's Island, with long accounts of years of solitary confinement, it did little to help.

When the weather cleared again I unpacked my fishing rod and carried it downstream a few miles, to a wide riffle that had opened up, the first big stretch of open water since early December. Below the riffle the old ice bulged up in blocky chunks against the still frozen river, but I studied the moving water, seeing an alternative to my chili diet. As a kid I'd fished hundreds of lakes, yet I really didn't know what to look for in fast water.

Even so, I'd brought a secret weapon—one of the night's mice. I'd been carrying on a limited battle with the rodents all winter, and with the sudden warming they were everywhere. I trapped them in droves.

As I stood beside the rushing flow of clear water I sank a hook through the entire mouse. I cast it out, letting it bob through the rapids to no avail. My only fishing experience was in Wisconsin, for vicious predators like northern pike, fish that wouldn't think twice about swallowing a mouse, or a squirrel, or probably small dogs. I wondered if the delicate and fabled trout would be different. I wondered how idiotic I was being, expecting them to come charging after an entire mouse. I wondered if their mouths even opened that wide. I didn't know a thing about them.

So I reeled in and I pulled the mouse apart, using only the brightly colored insides as bait. On my next cast I hooked a fish immediately. The fish ran wildly and for a moment I wasn't standing alone in three feet of snow beside a fifty-yard-long opening in river ice. I was back in the north woods, surrounded by my father and brothers, stunned by the first real fish I'd ever caught, a walleye, after years and years of hooking little panfish. I held down an urge to shout, "I got one!" as I had then.

The fish jumped over and over again, clearing the painful sparkles of the sun on the broken water, and I became unduly worried that it might get away. I cranked and cranked on my reel, bulling it through the water, running down as close to the bottom edge of the opening as I dared, trying to take the stress of the water's current off the line.

When I finally had the fish beside the bank I realized I couldn't reach in to lift it out. The snow created too steep a bank, the water too deep to step into. Holding my breath, I reached back on the rod and manhandled the fish out of the water, hoping the line and its lip would hold. The fish, a sixteen-inch cutthroat, flopped weakly on the clean bank of snow, large white crystals of the icy snow sticking to its curved side.

I cracked its head and held it up proudly, one of the few trout I'd ever caught, certainly the biggest. That fast I was able to forget the foolishness of casting an entire mouse and congratulate myself for having the smarts to discover mouse guts, a readily available bait. Another feast—a whole new season of feasting—was on its way.

I hooked a finger through the gills of the trout and started back for my tent. Soon I couldn't just walk in the warm, sunny air. I was so excited I began to jog, then finally sprint. The crust was still strong in the shade of the trees, and I cut into the deep timber, running as hard as I could possibly run, swerving through the branches, my moccasined feet as light as air.

I dashed across the rotten ice of Indian Creek, half expecting to crash through, but laughing at the risk, daring the world to try to get me. When I shot clear of the trees and into the rear of my meadow, where the sun had been working on the snow for hours, my feet crashed through the crust and I sprawled out, throwing my fishing rod out in front of me, out of harm's way. The trout slid off my finger too, skittering away across the snow. I was already laughing when Boone crashed into me, running right over my back, chasing the slippery fish. With the run and the laughter, I barely had the wind to call her back before she made off with my fish.

I tried cooking baked potatoes that afternoon, to complement my fish, and after banking the fire I crawled up Indian Ridge to the base of one of its huge ponderosas. I took off my shirts and stretched out in the open dirt there, dried already by the day of sun, and I soaked up the rays. I found a herd of ladybugs milling about in the pine needles and wondered where they had come from. They were bright and colorful in the brown dirt circled by white snow and I watched them until I was afraid I'd burned my potatoes down to hard, black raisins.

Beginning to establish a pattern, the rain resumed as soon as I grew used to the sunshine. I hiked through it, carried by the momentum of the bright days, but soon was spending more time in my tent, reading more and more of Papillon's solitary confinement. I wondered if I'd be able to handle anything like that.

The dawn before the first day of spring I lay in bed, knowing by the dim lighting of my tent that I was faced with another silent gray morning. Instead of throwing back the covers I lay there, studying the mildew stains in the dingy canvas roof of my tent. The stains made patterns, heads and faces, that by now I could trace blindfolded. The grayish light reminded me of the socked-in times of midwinter, long after the crystalline cold snaps had silenced the country. The midday light of the drizzly February avalanche weather had been just like this.

I tried to stop thinking of the months of cold and of the thaws, and I wondered if any ice had built up on the channel overnight. There hadn't been any ice-up lately, but chopping it was my only duty. So I lay in bed, looking at the mildew stains, wondering if the winter might not really be ending after all.

And then a cannon shot reverberated down my tight canyon. I sat upright and looked around, as if I could see a sound through the walls of my tent. There were often sonic booms back here, but this was not that.

It was as silent as ever after the shot and I was wondering if I really had heard anything. Then there was a rumble, soft crackings and groanings. I pushed up on my elbows and murmured the word "Ice." The river was opening up.

I dressed as I ran but when I reached the Selway it was over. The river was open. In the last few weeks small spots had been opening, but the ice that broke away jammed up at the first unopened spot. Along with the snow slides that had dammed the river, huge ice dams had formed, blocking the river and flooding some of my old trails.

The shot I'd heard had been the last upstream dam bursting after being hit by the rush caused by all the other broken dams farther upriver. Now large blocks of rotting ice battered against the rocks and slipped by and broke apart, or held up until other blocks slammed into them.

The air crackled with the sound. Not the grinding and bashing of the ice, but the sound of the river. The normal gurglings and hissings and rushes of moving water. My world was no longer silent. I remembered in the fall the noise had followed me everywhere, surrounding me. At night, as the lantern fluttered and died, the sounds would change to voices, or music—echoes of my father's symphonies, that wove through the darkness as I shivered waiting for the blankets to warm.

I stayed by the river all day, moving up and down stream, checking out old favorite spots, smiling stupidly, just listening. Walls of translucent blue ice with white snowcaps still hemmed in the water, but the river roared. Those voices had been buried all winter, under the ice and snow. Somehow, as I'd fished the one open stretch, I hadn't noticed their babble. I'd missed them without knowing it.

That night I lay in bed again, and as soon as the lantern sputtered and went out the voices took over, and I hummed along to the mysterious music I was so glad to have back.

It poured the day after the ice-out and I walked around by the river just to watch the water, the rain pocking its black surface even as the current raced along. I did some work at the channel, slipping boards into the headgate, reducing the amount of water entering the channel as Indian Creek rose. But I was soaked and cold in no time and I slogged back to my tent, settling in for a day of cooking, baking corn bread and rice pudding in the stove and a huge batch of chili on top.

It was a long, quiet day and I went to bed that night after dinner and one more long stint with my book.

I woke around two in the morning, an incredible pain knifing through my belly. I lay in the darkness, holding the flashlight I'd used to check the clock, and I waited for the cramps to subside. I was sweating hard and suddenly had to vomit and defecate at the same time. I stumbled out naked into the blackness and squatted in the soggy snow, knowing I didn't have a chance of making it the eighty yards to my outhouse. But, once outside, I couldn't make anything happen at either end and I crawled back into the tent. I was still covered in sweat but I stoked the fire anyway, not sure when I'd be able to do it again. Just that much work exhausted me, so much so that I considered pulling my blankets off the bed and curling up directly in front of the stove.

I slipped back into bed though, leaving the image of the fetal ball before the stove as a last resort, something I could still do if things got really bad.

I made more unsuccessful trips outside that night, spending

the time between trips sweating and trembling, knotted into a ball by the twisting squeeze inside me. By first light I finally managed to move my bowels, which seemed to only make matters worse, rather than bring any of the relief I'd hoped for. I'd tried to put it off, but now I brought my first-aid book to bed and read about appendicitis. The symptoms did not seem to match, but I couldn't put it out of my head. Lewis and Clark had lost one man. Only one in two years, over all those miles. Not to accident or Blackfeet, but to a ruptured appendix. I read the symptoms again, and told myself my appendix couldn't be exploding, and for comfort I flipped to the section on food poisoning. I had to breathe with my mouth open, taking short, panting breaths.

Regular food poisoning, the kind that lasted twenty-four hours, I read, could be caused by many things, the only one pertaining to me being eggs. I'd used several making the corn bread, and they were all five months old, from the food cache, but I'd been baking with them steadily since I'd been here.

Botulism, it continued, characterized by vomiting, stomach cramps and muscular weakness—and often fatal—was frequently caused by canned corn. I did have some of that for dinner, but I'd eaten half the can two days before, and had lived through that. I couldn't really be certain what was happening to me, if I'd be over it by tomorrow or not, or what I could do about it. The words 'often fatal' lay with me in the bed as the gray light of morning seeped through the canvas.

I remembered my boast to my parents—that if something bad happened I would simply have to walk out, or even crawl if I had to. I knew now that if whatever was happening to me was something that would kill me I wouldn't be doing any crawling. I would simply die.

The vomiting began early in the morning, racking my guts until I thought I was turning inside out. But afterward, lying back in bed exhausted, I felt a little better. By ten I managed to get myself dressed and totter all the way to the outhouse. I sat down shakily, glad to have made it this far. Hugh Glass had crawled hundreds of miles after his mauling. I hadn't been mauled, I'd just eaten dinner, and here I was delighted I'd made it eighty yards.

The morning staggered on, a routine of squatting in the snow and vomiting, clasping my sides in between, trying to keep myself from blowing up. By noon the sun came out and after a trip to the outhouse I felt a little better and decided I'd try walking to the channel, just to see if things there were all right, just to feel the sun a little longer. I pushed myself, running from the words 'often fatal,' thinking that if I could convince myself I felt better it would be a sure sign I had simple food poisoning. I doubted botulism would let me feel better before finishing me off. And if I had a ruptured appendix, I assured myself, I'd certainly be dead by now.

I sat down on the bridge over Indian Creek and saw that nothing had blocked the headgate overnight. I lay back and closed my eyes, then had to curl into a ball to ease my stomach cramps. For the first time ever I wondered if I would really die, and decided I probably wouldn't know about it if I did, sick enough to be more curious than scared. The smell of the creosote in the bridge timbers wrapped around me, its sharpness somehow pleasant, and I fell asleep for the first time that morning.

When I woke a full hour had passed and the sun was gone. The wind had picked up and I shuffled back to my tent just before the hail struck. I had to pin down the tent flaps with firewood and by the time I got back to my bed I was sweating and trembling again. But I hadn't thrown up for several hours, and that felt like some kind of achievement.

The storm passed quickly and by late afternoon I dragged myself outside again and lay down beneath a tree, the sun the only medicine I had. I brought my first-aid book with me, but didn't bother to open it. This was a wait-and-see game, nothing I could put a bandage on.

Soon another squall followed along, driving me back inside. I tried to read something light, lighter than first aid, but the pain made the words swim.

By evening the cramps began to subside and by night I was fairly sure I'd survive. But as the darkness settled in around me, I began to wonder. If I was truly deathly ill, an appendicitis or something, how would I make the decision that this was the real thing, that I had to make a move to survive? I thought I'd probably underestimate any illness. Accidents would be pretty straight forward—either the bleeding stops or it doesn't. Illness I knew far less about, and though I doubted it, I hoped that if the time came it would make itself obvious.

I could still remember my pride at hiking eighty yards to the outhouse and I fell back to sleep wondering what good it would really do to know that I was in mortal danger. I'd have to be able to make it at least the ten miles to the phone at Magruder. I wouldn't have a snowball's chance.

I didn't sleep much that night, but the next morning I felt pretty good—empty, but good. I ate tentatively, a piece of frying-pan bread, nothing more poisonous than flour, baking powder and water, and though I hated to do it, I threw out every bit of food I'd made before I got sick. Nothing was worth risking that again. From now on, I knew, I'd study each bit of food before using it, unable to tell a thing, but wondering what it held in store.

I got my strength and confidence back over the next few days and I was soon out hiking again, but I stayed fairly close to home, almost glad the drizzle returned, giving me a reason to hold to a routine of cooking and reading.

18

On the morning of the twenty-seventh of March I was into my last cup of coffee, caught up in *The Hound of the Baskervilles* and surrounded by the patter of rain on the canvas, when a sudden rip of shooting tore through my meadow. Six shots rang out as fast as someone could pull the trigger and I was out of my chair, crouched, wondering what to do before realizing there was only one person who might make an entrance like that.

Rader.

I poked my head out of the tent and saw Rader and Sponz on foot in the middle of my meadow, already beginning to laugh. I grabbed my black powder revolver and ran out into the meadow, waving it over my head and shouting, wishing it were loaded so I could return the salute.

We stood in the rain in the meadow and they tossed a bottle of whiskey to me, a holdover tradition from the mountain man book days. As I uncapped the bottle I realized these guys were still in those romantic book days. So was I, really, as soon as I was with them, and I tipped the bottle back for a choking swallow.

After we got through "How's it going?" I managed to ask them what in the world they were doing. What were they here for? How had they gotten in?

That set them to laughing again, and they had another snow

machine story to tell. This time they'd rented two, and they'd raced all the way in until they got to the slides. They'd snuck around some but had finally left their machines a few miles upriver and hiked in the last little ways. "Only crashed a dozen times or so," Rader said.

We walked back into the tent then and Rader picked up a piece of frying-pan bread I was about to have for breakfast. It wasn't pretty—a six-inch-wide disk, about an inch thick, variously browned and blackened, about the weight of a discus. Rib-sticking stuff. Rader weighed it in his hand and said, "Ah, another delicate pastry."

They asked what had been going on in here and I dug into my hiding place and retrieved the skin of the bobcat. Rader, who knew about such things, couldn't get over the size of it. It was worth a fortune, he told me, probably four hundred dollars. Two months' wages. I told the story of the cat's trip off the cliff, of his dragging himself toward me, and they marveled even more. I watched them admire the beautiful fur and wondered what it would feel like selling it, letting it go forever.

But finally, we sat down and I asked again what was going on. Were they just killing another long weekend?

Rader glanced at Sponz, grinning. He shook his head. "Getting married," he said. "Saturday."

He let that soak in a second before asking, "Wanna go?"

I glanced at one and then the other, and I knew they weren't kidding. "You really came in here to take me out?" I asked.

He nodded and I asked how it would work—when would I get back, how would I get back, all the logistics of it—and we sat around my little table and planned. Rader told me to grab the bobcat skin and within half an hour we were back at their machines, piling on. I held Boone across my lap, pinned against Rader's back, before I really had a chance to realize what I was doing or where I was going.

We tipped over on nearly every slide, until I started walking even the easiest looking ones. Our ribs ached before we reached Magruder, laughing so hard at each other as we'd pick ourselves out of the snow and set the machine back on its skis. We didn't have a clue what we were doing. And, for once, there was no one here to see that.

Once we turned up Deep Creek toward the pass, the slides gave out and we had smooth sailing. It was an odd feeling to skate past the landmarks up to the pass, shooting by places like Slow Gulch and Blondie's, places I hadn't seen since December, when I'd chased after my dad and brother. As we passed the places I told Rader the stories and he'd shake his head, asking if I was kidding. I started to feel better about those desperate days. Maybe now I finally had a story of my own, something I could tell about, something I could wow my friends with. Suddenly though, I wondered if it was worth it, worth what my dad and brother had gone through. I wasn't sure, and I doubted I'd tell many people more than a few of those stories. It wasn't something that could be understood right off.

On the down side of the pass, back in Montana at last, Sponz shot by us, hotdogging. He zoomed out of sight and it was nearly a mile before we saw him again, staggering around on the road, looking for his snow machine, his cap crunched down, nearly covering his dazed eyes.

We dismounted and rounded him up and sat him down. We found his snow machine off the road, nearly buried beneath a tree. He'd been bounced off on a divot and the machine had driven itself off the road. By the time he got up, punch-drunk from landing on his head, he could not guess where it had possibly gone. Once we figured he was probably going to be OK we chugged on, a lot slower than before, keeping each other in sight.

When we reached the Deerslayer we loaded the machines onto the rented trailer and took off. I could hardly believe how fast everything went. We'd covered a hard two-day walk in a few hours. Rushing up out of Darby I looked off to the west and saw Trapper Peak, still heavy under its snow. Finally I was seeing its other side, from the Bitterroot Valley, and in little more than an hour we were back in Missoula.

We stopped at Sponz's first, where I took a shower. It was such a far cry from my miserable little sponge baths that I stayed in until

Sponz asked if I'd gone down the drain. He sat on the toilet, filling in stories while I steamed. When the hot water finally ran out I had to borrow his clothes. Out here the layers upon layers of wool and my knee-high moccasins only served to draw stares.

Sponz and Rader were both beat from the day of snowmobiling and we went to bed early. Rader went to his apartment, taking Boone with him because dogs weren't allowed in Sponz's room. I slept on Sponz's floor.

The next day started with a call from Rader, telling me that he'd let Boone out in the morning and she was gone. While Rader said he'd put messages around and call the radio stations I picked at the gluey edge of the emergency number sticker on the phone, thinking of Boone howling through the night at the Paradise lion camp. "OK," I said, hanging up. There really wasn't anything else we could do. She'd never been out in Missoula before, and there was no particular place we could look. We drove around for a few hours anyway, without seeing a trace of her. I walked through campus, an open place full of dogs that I thought might attract her. But I kept bumping into friends and soon the party grew unavoidable. I let myself go with my friends, hoping for a phone call from whoever might find Boone.

The next several days fell into a pattern as steady as the routines I'd made to kill time in my early days in the Selway. In the morning, at first light, I'd walk alone through the quiet town, searching for Boone, wondering what she was going through. I crossed the bridge over the Clark Fork, the river bigger and farther away than I was used to. I saw ducks and felt naked without the rifle on my shoulder. I dropped down to the river and searched there for Boone, turning corners hoping to see her charging back to me through the snow and brush, as she would after a deer chase had been impossible to resist. But there wasn't any snow here, and Boone didn't charge around any corners.

As each day passed into night my time was taken up by all the people who'd spent weeks sending me off in the fall. I had a dinner date with a girl I'd met shortly before going off to the woods, and once in the restaurant I couldn't get over the number of people, so closely spaced. I grew uncomfortable standing in line at the salad bar, not used to people standing behind me, not used to having to watch out for anyone besides myself. In the Selway every glance of movement meant something—something was there, something was happening. Here it was just movement, everywhere.

Back at the table I studied the line, realizing it was just a line, that no one here had sinister intentions. I noticed the tight jeans the men wore, the stars cut into their back pockets. They wouldn't last a second in the mountains, and they'd soak up water like a wick, freezing whoever wore them. At the same time I knew it didn't make any difference, that they'd never be worn there.

I felt funny about being waited on, about having everything set before me all ready to eat, without having to lift a finger myself. But I got over that as soon as I started my salad. I'd forgotten how badly I missed fresh food.

After the dinner we walked through the night looking for Boone, my date as worried about her as I was. I thought of Beau, Brian's dog, lost on his first lion trail in the mountains. I wondered what Boone was trailing on her first trip out of the mountains. At least there were no coyotes here.

The wedding went fairly smoothly, though Rader and I didn't sleep the night before it. Sponz saved the day by hauling Rader through a shower and dressing him in time for the ceremony. I stood in the background, my borrowed suit tight around my neck and shoulders, woozy from the endless late nights, still trying to watch everything, the two of them at the altar, wondering when this had all happened, how they had gone from a date or two to marriage in what seemed, now that I was out, to be hardly any time at all. As the priest rattled on I worried about Boone.

The party rolled on through the weekend and I rolled with it, stunned by all there was to see, by all the people and all the talking. I told a few stories about what it was like back in the Selway, but I grew quiet in the crowds, leaning back against walls, trying to keep my eye on all the movement. The Selway wasn't the easiest thing to describe and these people were the same people I had left, full into the college party crowd, masters of fun without thought.

There was no word of Boone.

The Monday after the wedding things settled down. The college kids went back to class and the parents went home. Rader and I went down to Pacific Hide and Fur with the bobcat skin. I'd never seen a fur buyer and I watched as he fluffed out the pelt, measuring, pointing out invisible flaws.

He put on a show before making his first offer—four hundred and twenty dollars. I was a little startled, but already I'd begun to have second thoughts. When the buyer began to talk about tagging and licenses, bitching about the hoops the Fish and Game made him jump through, I became less and less certain that I wanted to sell the skin.

Finally, when the buyer determined we didn't have a tag, Rader took over, getting the guy to admit they had ways around it—although he also said that they sure wouldn't pay premium price for the risk. How close to premium, Rader wanted to know, and the buyer thought maybe he could risk one hundred and fifty bucks.

That tore it. I picked up the skin, beautifully fluffed and combed by the buyer's expert hand, and we headed out. I thought of the old cat, hanging on to the deer's back, his teeth too worn to finish his kill, refusing to give up even as the deer ran off the cliff, even as I approached his shattered body with a rock, turning to swipe at Boone with his claws out and ready. There was no point in selling it. Anyone who saw it afterward would only see pretty fur. I didn't need money so badly it was worth killing the cat's story.

Rader tried coming up with alternate plans, and I played along rather than trying to explain that I wasn't going to sell it. He was married now, and had to worry about money and security and things like that. And he hadn't seen the fierce yellow slits of the bobcat's eyes. We walked back to campus for Rader's class and I switched the subject rather than going into any of that. It seemed a thing a person would either see or not see.

After dropping Rader off I started my hopeless rounds of the campus, searching through the dogs for Boone. I bumped into another friend in the central oval and as we were talking he suddenly looked over my shoulder and said, "Hey, isn't that your dog?"

I spun around in time to see Boone trotting toward me, smiling the way dogs do, as if she'd just come back from one of her little tours around our meadow. She'd been gone four days. We rumbled through the center of the campus, tearing up the soggy grass.

Once Boone showed up I was ready to go back in to the Selway. I had the fish to worry about and I was tired of imposing on people out here, staying at Sponz's, hanging out with Rader the newlywed. I was tired of drinking and talking. I wanted just to sit in my tent.

No one could afford renting two machines again, or even the trailer to haul them on, so Rader and I borrowed a disintegrating truck and limped it down to Hamilton where we rented a single machine. We pushed it into the back of the truck and by noon were at the end of the plowed road, thirty-five miles from my tent. It was a warm, sunny day, the snow already slick on top, crusted hard below. We'd had one more going-away party that couldn't be beat the night before, the same as in the fall, and we were both tired, feeling pretty puny.

We got the machine fired up and started for the pass. The snow was sticky beneath the slush, grabbing at the skis, and within a mile the machine lost its power. We jettisoned Boone but she was able to keep up with us in an easy trot.

Within another few hundred yards the machine just stopped. The engine would race, but we would not move. Rader and I got off and looked at each other. We opened the cowling and saw that the belt was still there. That's about all he'd learned to repair. "Might've burned a hole in the cylinder," he said.

The man in the rental shop had warned about that, about the tough snow conditions, about trying to haul two people around. He'd recognized Rader, seemed to recall something of the battered machines he'd returned before, but not quite enough.

We let the engine cool, Rader sitting on the black vinyl seat while I dropped down into a snowdrift, comfortable back in my layers of wool. We talked some, finally alone, not drinking, making sense. We talked mostly of marriage, which was a new thing, something unknown, as hard to comprehend as my winter in here had been for me in the fall. Frightening for the same reasons.

When we decided the engine was cool we started it up again and Rader ran it another two hundred yards up the road while I walked along beside. It wasn't going to make it.

We sat down in the snow again.

He could drive me back to Missoula, but he couldn't really afford to take off more time for another shot at bringing me back. We couldn't afford another rental, even if the guy would be willing to let us kill another machine. I said I thought I couldn't afford to be away from my fish any longer. A tree could fall across the channel. A blizzard could strike. Anything.

We sat there, beginning to avoid one another's eyes. "It's already one o'clock," he said.

We hadn't eaten anything that day, hangovers spoiling our appetite.

"You don't have a sleeping bag, do you?" he asked, though the answer was obvious. I didn't have a pack.

I shook my head. "No food either."

"Or snowshoes?"

I shook my head again.

"How much sleep did you get last night?"

We both started to smile. "About an hour, I guess."

"Well, what are you waiting for? See you later."

We laughed at that, but I told him I thought I really would walk back in. He didn't think it was a good idea, and he was right, but I didn't want to go back to Missoula. I didn't want to arrive at Sponz's step to announce he hadn't gotten rid of me yet. I didn't want Rader to have to explain to Lorrie that he had to try to take me down again. I'd worn Missoula out and I was ready to get back home.

I assured Rader that I could stop at Blondie's or Slow Gulch if things got bad and we stood up. "You sure?" he asked, and I nodded. We shook hands and he sputtered the machine through a circle. "Goes great downhill," he said.

"Great."

"Good luck," he called, and as he crept back down the road, I started to slog uphill, toward the pass and the Selway, and eventually Indian Creek.

Within an hour the sun had softened the snow so that in the open southwest switchbacks my feet broke through the crust at nearly every step. The snow was heavy enough that I'd only sink to my knee, unlike the hip-deep plunges of the powder months, but it was slow, tough, maddening progress.

Up high the sun on the snow was dazzling and my eyes began to water, the night's headache resurfacing behind them. I wondered how quickly snow blindness struck. I'd been picked up on a rainy day and my sunglasses were back at my tent.

To top it all off, Boone had gone into heat, beginning to bleed. She'd walk a little ways, then drag her rear in the snow, whimpering. I didn't know much about that, and I wondered if she'd gotten a load of pups while she'd been out painting the town on her own.

I still felt pretty good by the time I made the pass. At least it was downhill the rest of the way. But I was hungry now, and Magruder was still fourteen miles way. I stopped at Blondie's, feeling tired, from sleeplessness more than anything. I wanted to stop, but I couldn't imagine what I'd do then. It was still light out and I had no food to eat, or bed to sleep in. I pushed on, sucking mouthfuls of snow now and then.

I didn't have a watch or even my wind-up clock, and I spent a lot of time looking at the sun, wondering how much light I had left. I didn't have a flashlight either, and I tried to remember what the moon was doing, but in the city I'd paid no attention, and I didn't know if I'd have any light at all.

Trudging past all the landmarks of my search for Paul and Dad brought up some of those memories, but mostly I had Missoula on my mind, and the wild ride out last week on the snow machines. I couldn't yet quite believe how anxious I was to get back in here, to get out of Missoula. I put one foot in front of the other, over and over again, wondering how I'd spent all winter hanging on the hope of getting out for a few days. What had I been thinking?

I stumbled on in a daze, finally reaching Magruder just as it got too dark to see what I was doing. I was as played out as I'd ever been, too beat to even turn on the propane. I found a can of apricots in the cellar and ate them. After stoking the furnace I sat down on the heating vent, waiting for the fire to take hold, driving away the chill of my drying sweat.

For the first time Magruder didn't seem very deluxe. It was only a rest point. If I hadn't been so exhausted I would have pushed on to Indian Creek. I'd even considered it, when I reached the Selway. After twenty-five miles, the last ten to my tent seemed like a pretty short hop, a path I knew every inch of, and I'd been going on auto-pilot for quite a while already. But I had just enough sense left to see how foolish that would be, and I put it off for the morning.

As soon as I was warm and dry I crawled into a couple of sleeping bags and passed out. I woke in the morning with a mouse pulling at my beard, and after checking to make sure the fire was out, I made the final trudge. Before noon I was back home. I thought I'd be famished, but after checking the channel and finding everything there to be fine, Boone and I walked up the side of Indian Creek and stretched out in the baked dry dirt beneath a ponderosa and fell sound asleep.

19

As soon as I had my camp and the channel squared away from my long absence I crunched over the hard frozen snow to the top of Indian Ridge. Once up top, I strapped on the snowshoes I'd left up there and strode on. I walked until I could see Trapper Peak guarding the Bitterroot Valley, and I perched on a rock and stared. It looked better from this side, something in the distance, something impossible to see too clearly, something I could make perfect in my mind.

I stayed up top all day, looping back to the point of Indian Ridge just before dusk. I hung my snowshoes back in their tree and slogged through the sloppy brown mud and rock fragments of the southwest slope toward home.

Rain closed back in soon afterward, mixed with snow in the mornings, and I stayed in my tent tending to any chores I could think of. In one of my Angier books I came across directions for making a hunting sling—not a slingshot, but a sling, like the one David used so effectively against Goliath.

I cut the leather pouch and the thongs and tied them together, then stepped into the drizzle to give it a try.

Picking up a stone the size of a robin's egg, I twirled it over my head, three times, just like the book said. Then I released one of the thongs. The stone shot off into the trees—behind me. I laughed and walked farther from my tent, out of range, before picking up another stone. Soon I was sending stones whizzing in every possible direction, occasionally even near where I wanted them to go. By the time my arm felt as if it might drop off I had the technique down solidly enough that I could usually throw a stone forward, rather than backward. If Goliath had strolled into my meadow I would have been in a world of hurt.

I worked with the sling every day, ambling through the drizzle close to home. I'd sizzle stones into the rising river currents, eventually even bouncing some off the rocks I aimed at.

But, even though the rain did not let up, my energy seemed to grow with every day of spring. The snow in the meadow began to disappear, only the hard-packed paths of my trails hanging on, skinny white lines showing where I'd walked all winter. One evening a pair of mergansers appeared in the wide stretch of river above my tent, the stretch the moose had crashed through. Their brightly white and black breeding plumage shone as they skipped across the water like stones, heads beneath the surface in a feeding frenzy. I'd nearly forgotten such creatures would be returning.

I kept on hiking, rain or shine. The calls of the ruffed and blue grouse boomed through the woods, so low it was hard to tell if I heard or felt them. I began to see bear tracks regularly and every day I crossed paths with herds and herds of deer and usually a group or two of elk, though the elusive bighorn remained just that. Elk antlers lay scattered through the woods like chaff and I dragged the most impressive racks home with me, building a pile I didn't have any use for. The antlers were somehow fascinating, and I carried them home just because I couldn't leave them lying around where I'd never see them again.

Coming back down Indian Creek one evening, lugging a huge matched pair of seven-point elk antlers I'd found more than half a mile apart, I glanced up at a small black speck swinging through the sky. I stopped and watched as the speck grew in size, diving down until it had grown into an eagle. It kept coming, wings tucked like those of a falcon, screaming into full size, its head and tail gleaming white in the high haze.

I looked for what it might be stooping at but could see nothing. Just before I thought it would crash into the trees it opened its wings and swung into a screeching turn, climbing wildly with the built up speed. As its momentum ebbed it slowed, tucking its wings back into its body. Finally it stalled completely, hanging motionless for an instant before tumbling over on its back, into another stoop, its speed building again until it swooped back into the sky, nearly scraping the trees. I watched as it stooped over and over, then finally caught a thermal and circled upward, climbing completely out of sight. I whooped, unable to keep quiet when something played so wildly so close by. The eagle looked exactly as I felt.

When the weather broke a scattering of small, sky-blue butterflies began to appear, hugging the ground and scattering around my legs as I walked. Boone never tired of chasing them. I started to cook outside, rather than remaining cooped up in the hot, smoky tent, and I lay on the ground waiting for dinner, watching ants and heavy, round-bodied, iridescent green flies crawling on the damp earth. Tiny wildflowers, specks of yellow and blue, popped up everywhere. I was surprised how little of this I had realized had been missing all winter.

More mergansers returned, and a pair of goldeneyes. Then real ducks started to move through. Teal first, green-winged. I stalked them without a trace of success. I was used to grouse, which would watch with interest as I aimed my rifle at them. The ducks winged away as soon as they caught a glimpse of me, rifle still on my shoulder.

As the water in the creeks and rivers continued to rise, beginning to carry dirt and silt along with it, my work around the channel increased slightly. I had to shut the flow down as much as I could. The silt the creek carried from the runoff was heavy enough to bury the salmon in the rocks where they hid. I put a screen in the end of the channel, which was actually a crude holding tank. If the salmon started to make their move they would pool up there until I could count them and release them.

But no salmon appeared.

The weather turned fine for several days and I began to take even longer hikes. If it was above forty or forty-five degrees I often tied my shirts around my waist. I wondered if I'd really forgotten it would ever get warm again. One day it hit sixty and I staggered awestruck through the heat.

I finally found a way around the cliffs I'd nearly fallen off of earlier and I made my way to Sheep Creek, searching the wide drainage there for bighorn. The sides of the draw were treeless, already green in the rush of water from the melt-off, dotted with broken chunks of gray boulders. Once I spotted a herd of nearly fifteen sheep, but it was late and they were so far away I couldn't actually be sure they weren't deer. I turned for home, still hoping to find a bighorn up close. I'd never seen one in the wild.

I found bear scat in my meadow one morning and, stooped over the blackish clot, I glanced quickly around the dark trees surrounding me. My tent was loaded with bear delectables like peanut butter and honey. I went in and loaded my muzzleloader, wondering what it would sound like if I had to shoot a bear inside my tent in the middle of some horrifying night. And, remembering how slowly it had affected the moose, I wondered if it would do any good.

I began to search for bear on my walks, never having seen any of them in the wild either. I found more scat, and tracks—even scarred saplings they'd torn up scratching away their thick winter coats, the naked branches sticky with sap, long hair clinging everywhere. After inspecting one such tree I walked more stealthily, sure the bear was nearby. When I popped my head over the next rise I was twenty yards from a huge mule deer. I was so set on the idea of finding a bear I nearly gasped, sure for an instant that I'd stumbled on what I was looking for.

The deer didn't run. Instead it stood tense, its ears swiveling for sound, its nose twitching. It shifted its weight nervously, then took a step. Toward me. It took another and I wondered what was going on. It kept coming at me and for a moment I wondered if a deer could be dangerous. I hadn't moved and Boone was stone still by my side.

The deer came to within ten yards, then veered suddenly, giving an odd, huffing bark. It bounced down the hill in its jarring, stiff-legged bound, then stopped, its nose high in the air. It was nearly around me then and my scent, or Boone's, was clear in the air. The deer was gone in a streak.

I followed after it, smiling, wanting to see where it would go once over the rise before me, when it knew I couldn't see it. I wanted to know if it would continue straight on, or loop around, or just stop. I glanced across the draw, checking for any trace of bear, then crept up the ridge to peek over for the deer.

What I saw instead were bighorns. Almost tawny, much lighter than deer, they grazed single file into the wind away from me, the closest thirty yards away. Two of them lifted their heads now and then, checking below them before continuing to graze. It was several seconds before the last in line lifted his heavy head and peered down the slope. Before dropping back to feed he glanced over his shoulder. His gaze stopped dead on my face.

His jaw hung in midchew and he brought his legs up solidly beneath him. He turned in a little stiff-legged shuffle until facing me head on. The others grazed on a few moments more before the largest sheep glanced back and saw the twitching legs and fixed glare of my sheep. He whirled around then, startling the others, and in a clatter of loose rock all the sheep were suddenly facing me, all rams, their faces, framed by their strange horns, intent on mine. Watching their battering ram heads all pointing my way, I remembered wondering if a deer could be dangerous. If these sheep charged I wouldn't land until I was back down on the Selway.

Suddenly there was a scuffle above me and a smaller ram burst down the hill, straight through the group before me. That was all any of them needed and they cascaded down the hill behind the smallest ram, straight away from me. I stood still, grinning as the last white rump disappeared around the curve of hill.

Searching for bear, chasing deer, and finally the mythical bighorn pops out of nowhere, right in my own backyard.

It seemed as if there were no end to the animals. On my way home that evening through the dense woods on the creek I was startled out of my wits by a rushing blur at head level. I ducked in time to see a goshawk lumbering down the trail, trying frantically to avoid crashing into me without dropping the squirrel in his talons. In a second he was gone, flitting between branches so thick I wouldn't have guessed anything could fly through them, leaving me with my heart beginning to race, too late as usual.

I hiked and hiked and the days grew longer but I wished for days longer still. It seemed there wasn't nearly enough time to see everything I needed to see. Up high I would sit and watch the storms come in, the clouds tearing apart on the saw-toothed ridge backs. Now and then I had to hide beneath trees as berserk hailstorms flew over. I'd laugh then, as the deafening roar of the hail and wind made even my own laughter impossible to hear, and I'd cuff at Boone at the wildness of it all. By the time the storm passed we would be rumbling in the crunching balls of ice that would disappear as soon as the sun tore back through the ragged clouds.

But even though my excitement was barely containable I still had to eat, and to eat I had to cook. I'd neglected that while I spent all my time out in the hills and I was finally down to the bitter end of everything. I had to take a day off to bake loaves of bread and pots of beans and delicacies like rice pudding and coffee cake.

The heat from the baking fire drove me out of my tent, but I could not wander away. Every hour I had to punch down the rising dough, pull another taste treat out of the oven. I remembered Rader laughing at my frying-pan bread, and when I pulled a perfect loaf of French bread out of the battered old stove I wished he could see me now.

Finally the only thing left to cook was dinner itself, a blue grouse I'd found on the top of the ridge, booming out his low, rumbling call. A few weeks before I'd shot a squirrel and when gutting it I'd discovered it was pregnant. I'd killed six squirrels with one shot, and I hadn't shot any squirrels after that. I'd been letting the grouse go for the same reason, but by his booming I knew this one was a male and I hadn't been able to resist.

While I waited for my feast to roast I sat in the remnants of my woodpile, soaking up the last of the sun and searching for ticks, another of the animals that had reappeared with the spring. I'd just pulled off my shirt when I heard a rumble. I sat up on my stump and turned to the end of my meadow as the noise became deafening. It wasn't long before a yellow snowplow lumbered into view, followed by a Forest Service truck.

I stared. Except for the snowslides, the road had been clear of snow for almost a week. The plow lumbered on but the pickup stopped and a Forest Service employee I had met in the fall came out; we shook hands and talked a bit. It had taken them a week to open the road and he raged about what a bitch the slides had been to cut through. As if it were the snowslides' fault, or maybe even mine.

They wanted to get clean through to Paradise, the end of the road, and back out before dark, so he didn't stay long. They were opening the road for the bear hunters, he said, who pushed for an earlier and earlier opening each year.

I thanked them for stopping and went back into my tent to think. I was still there a few hours later when they roared out, beeping their horns.

The road was open. I could drive around now. To Paradise, or to Magruder for a bath. I could even drive clear out to Montana, to Missoula. I could go anywhere I wanted. It was an odd feeling and I didn't know what to make of it. I didn't know if I wanted to go anyplace. I was afraid I might miss something in here.

After all winter of wishing to get out for a few days I didn't hop in my truck and go. I stayed in the mountains, watching the spring come in, changing everything I knew.

20

It snowed hard the day after they opened the road, but the next day heated right back up and within days of the road's opening I began to have visitors. Lots of Forest Service people came in, seemingly for little reason. The wardens came back too, staying a little longer now that they could drive around anywhere they liked. They all had horror stories of how rough the pass was, still nothing more than two wheel ruts through the snow, but they kept coming anyway. I even saw Brian, the lion hunter, and we had a drink together. He was gearing up the Paradise outfitter camp for the influx of bear hunters.

But now that we weren't bundled up to our eyeballs against the cold, and now that everybody could just pop over the pass without a thought, a difference between the outsiders and me became apparent. They were clean. They weren't the lion hunters who stayed in for weeks at a time. The Forest Service guys and the wardens wore spotless, ironed uniforms. Even Brian looked less rough in his light clothes and shampooed hair.

I looked like I lived in a cave.

The first nice afternoon I had I hauled my washtub out beside my tent and stoked the stove full to bursting, setting the big pot on top. As usual, it took hours to heat the water, but I was able to stay out of the sweltering tent this time, and when I poured the water over my head in the sunlight it felt quite a bit more luxurious than it had in the dark of my tent with the below-zero drafts eddying around me.

I danced around naked in the sun, drying off, but before long I began to imagine I could hear the distant rumble of truck engines and I dodged into the tent for my clothes. Turned out I had just imagined them, but sitting on the stump in front of my tent, my freshly washed hair still damp, I began to realize that this place was no longer mine alone.

The weather kept improving, even hitting seventy one day, a temperature I was certain I'd never see on the Forest Service thermometers. Wildflowers sprang up everywhere as the snow melted and I walked around with a wildflower guide my sister Ellen had sent in. Trillium came in just before the dogtooth violets and now spring beauty and ground nut were overrunning my meadow. Large, dark butterflies with yellow or white wing borders, along with smaller orange and black dappled species, added themselves to the clouds of the tiny sky-blue ones that had been around nearly since the melt-off.

I even saw a snowshoe hare, its white coat already gone completely to gray.

And, for the first time since my job began, I finally saw my fish. They began to leave their hideout in the rocks to start their long swim. They were about an inch long, pinkish with dark vertical splotches down their sides. A scrap of red yolk sac still bulged from their bellies. They were too small to do anything, let alone swim eighteen hundred miles. I felt sorry for them.

They schooled up in the pool below the falls I'd chopped ice off of all winter, some of them so weak that the current through the screen pressed them against the mesh and they couldn't swim off. They died there.

I counted the living in a glass measuring cup, putting in an ounce of water and adding fish one at a time until I had two ounces. They averaged one hundred and ten fish to the ounce. Hardly keepers. I began to release them daily from the pool. Soon I was releasing fifteen hundred a morning.

The trout, of course, went wild. A few salmon would slip by the holding tank, enough to keep the trout lined up at the channel exit, waiting. One morning I even found two ambitious cutthroat in the holding pool. They must have squeezed through the headgate and wriggled the entire length of the channel, through an inch of water, and thrown themselves over the waterfall at the top of the pool. I had them for breakfast. They were stuffed with my tiny salmon.

I had always understood why there were two and a half million eggs in the channel. I'd understood the reproductive strategy of the salmon—a swarming method, flooding the waterways with more fish than could possibly be consumed. But seeing the opened trout bellies, spilling salmon fry and fry parts, I really knew what that strategy entailed. After surviving the harrowing ice of winter, the tiny fish had been set up for a massacre.

After the first rush of traffic the open road appeared to lose its novelty and things began to settle down again. I still hiked all day after releasing my fish, not wishing to be caught in my tent where I'd have to talk to anyone who might drop by. Up top I was alone and now, instead of going just for the sun, I went for the snow, a reminder of the long winter so rapidly disappearing.

The road had been open for a couple of weeks, and after spending another day all on top, on snowshoes, I slid down the mud of the old Nez Perce trail as evening closed in. I hit the Selway at the ford and started up the road the last four miles to my tent. It was nearly dark, but with the road wide open I'd been easing my rules about being home before dark.

Soon I heard engines. I stepped out of the road and at the last second dropped back into the bushes with Boone. We watched two trucks go by, Texas plates, headlights on, two people to a truck, guns in the racks. I scratched Boone's ears. The bear hunters had arrived.

When the trucks were gone I walked on slowly in the darkness. I wasn't happy to see all these strangers. It was hardly fair that after all winter people could just drive in here, like it was nothing. This wasn't just some place you could come into to blast a bear or two. It wasn't just that.

I remembered how much fun I'd had in the fall with the few hunters who had invited me into their camps. I'd been embarrassed to talk to them, because they seemed to know so much about all this mountain stuff. Now there were more hunters coming in and I didn't want them.

They didn't know anything about this place. They didn't know about skiers turned back at the pass, or about nights at forty below with the stars so sharp they seemed within reach. They didn't know that snow had sat here four feet deep for months, that the dregs of snow they saw in the meadows were my winter trails, hardpacked, still lingering despite the sun. They would see it as it was now, without knowing what it had gone through to get like this. That was not right. I felt like I had paid my dues, and now freeloaders were driving in for what I'd earned.

When I passed Raven Creek, where the bobcat had died, things didn't seem any more fair. I walked out the last two miles and when I entered my meadow and found the two trucks parked by my tent I sat down in the trees, waiting for them to leave before I crossed the dark clearing.

The following morning I'd just started walking to the channel when the trucks returned, driving upriver from Paradise. I was trapped this time, and they unloaded from their trucks, a pair of husbands and wives. They came down the hill to the channel and me.

They introduced themselves and we shook hands. One of the women went nuts over Boone, squatting down and stroking her head, ooing and aahing about how pretty she was. Boone had grown into a large, handsome dog, mostly shepherd, with some husky showing through. She was barrel chested from the miles she had covered, up and down mountains, throughout her puppyhood. Now she sat beside me, unsure of what to make of strangers.

The men said the rangers at West Fork had told them I'd been here all winter, and if anyone knew where the bears were, it would be me. They said they'd waited half the night for me at my tent.

They were somewhat interested in the fish, and in my winter, and they drove their trucks back to my tent as I walked. I gave them coffee and all they wanted to know about was bears.

As little as I wanted them to be impressed with my winter I was somehow put out by the way they brushed over it. I told them I hadn't seen any bears. They didn't believe that. They had done their homework. The Selway was crawling with bears. In fact, it was one of the few areas where a hunter was allowed to kill two.

They finally figured I was trying to keep all the bears for myself and they laughed about that. The woman never left Boone alone and I think Boone enjoyed the attention. Actually they were pretty nice people. I just wasn't ready for anyone to get my country handed to them on a platter.

I saw these people nearly every day. They'd stop with iced beers in their coolers and want to know where I had seen the bears. I'd tell them where, if it was more than six or seven miles from the road. They'd laugh then, and say they didn't have horses. I'd laugh too.

More hunters came in, and the guides returned with their own. These were all the cat hunters of the winter and I was glad to see them. We tuned it up a few nights in their tents, with the gas lanterns hissing and the clients shoved a little to the side while we traded winter stories.

One morning Brian skidded to a halt beside my tent, slamming his door viciously. I was out whittling a new ramrod for my rifle and Brian charged over, jerking a thumb back at his truck, where two hunters sat looking at the dashboard. They'd been driving down the road, Brian said, looking for bear sign, when they'd spotted a bear itself, shuffling through the thick stuff across the river. Before he could stop him, one of the hunters had leapt out and shot at the bear.

"He hit him too," Brian said. "But I don't know how good."

Brian had chewed him out, asking him how the hell he planned to cross the river to get it, how he thought they'd bring it back even if he had killed it? The hunter had been excited, and hadn't thought of that.

Brian and I walked down and looked at the river, which was still on the rise, looking bigger and angrier every day. "This is the best place I could think to cross," Brian said. I went through the river in my mind and had to agree.

During the winter I'd told Brian something about my swimming. He'd said he wasn't much of a swimmer. Now he asked if I felt like going over with him. I said, "Sure," but looking at the race of water I knew being able to swim wouldn't make much difference.

We cut staffs and Brian tied his rifle across his shoulders. Then we stepped into the water and began shuffling across, leaning heavily upstream against our sticks. Before I was halfway across my feet and legs were completely numb and every time I lifted a foot the current swept it downstream. Without the staffs we wouldn't have had a chance.

Once across we sat down and rubbed at our legs. The pain was lip-biting sharp as the feeling returned. We swore and grinned at each other and started up the bank to get the blood pumping again.

Within an hour we were at the sight of the shooting, a torn-up area in the undergrowth by the river. Blood flecks spotted a few leaves and some of the saplings were snapped off clean, where the bear had bitten in rage. We glanced around and Brian took his rifle off his shoulder. I had a hatchet in my belt and I took that out. I laughed at the idea of fending off a bear with it. More Hugh Glass idiocy.

We trailed the bear for more than a mile but the blood got thinner and then gave out all together. Finally we couldn't find the trail anymore and Brian swore again about the hunters. I thought of the bear, shot somewhere, its roly-poly gait maybe slowed by a carried paw, and then of the hunters, waiting in the truck, complete strangers to this place.

Brian and I tried to cross the river twice before we were forced to give up and hike back to my tent and cross there. Brian said thanks and without saying a word to his hunters jumped into his truck, soaking wet, and roared off.

I had one visit from nonhunters, a young couple in a Honda. They'd been reading their map in some peculiar way and thought they were on a shortcut to Idaho. I couldn't help but laugh. They'd made Idaho all right, but it was a hell of a way from here to Boise.

They stayed a day and a half, hiking up to the top with me, where we shot a blue grouse for dinner. He was a chef someplace and he cooked the grouse like someone who knew how. It was quite a treat from the single way I'd fixed them all winter.

I liked those two. They reminded me of myself seven months earlier. They didn't pretend they knew anything about these mountains. Happy ignorants, without the pretense of knowledge that had come to seem a prerequisite to hunting here.

But if Hondas were making it in, everybody would soon be driving in. And that's what happened. I began to get weekend crowds—people anxious to do anything, even just a long, rough drive, after the cold, holed-up winter. The road, which had only been uncovered from four feet of snow for a month, began to grow rutted with their tracks.

Eventually I drove out to Missoula. My friends were all still there and we had another round of parties that tried to rival those in the fall, but the desperation wasn't in it for me anymore. I wasn't afraid to go away. In fact, I wanted to go back, only afraid now that Indian Creek was no longer what it had come to be. Now, it seemed, it was anybody's.

While I was out I made a call to Nevada, where I had my Park Service lifeguarding job waiting for me. Yes, they said, they could use me early. I called Idaho Fish and Game and talked to the warden. He said he thought they could get someone to spend the last few weeks releasing the last of the fish. It was no problem finding someone to do it for a few weeks in the spring, he said. Nothing like getting someone to commit to an entire winter.

I went back to Indian Creek. There were two new tents in my meadow, bright green and orange affairs. I drove past them and disappeared into my tent. It was still spring, just the middle of May, but the real spring, the opening of the mountains after the winter burial, was gone now. I couldn't stay around and watch all these strangers come in one after another.

I climbed up Indian Ridge a last time with Boone. For a long time I sat under the tree I'd hung my snowshoes on all spring. I scratched Boone's ears and tried not to think of what I would do with her. In my brief trips to Missoula I'd discovered that Boone had been brought into the woods too early. She didn't have a clue about city life. She didn't hang by me in town like she did in the woods, and on my last trip in she'd spent another day out on her own, lost. She also had a tendency to chase cars from the front as if, like deer, they would turn and run from her. The Park Service didn't allow dogs in seasonal housing either, but I couldn't picture Boone tied up anyway, waiting at the end of a length of chain for my days of work to end.

Finally I stood, thumping her side and taking one more look at everything from up here. The mountains lined out as far as I could see. There were the big, burned-over hills to the northwest, still open and bare from the fire in the forties. Due west was the giant cirque that had filled with blue ice after a freak rain last fall. The needle-littered dirt beneath me still had that fresh, heavy smell to it, the one the winter had made me forget was possible. At last I took my snowshoes from the branches and strapped them across my back. Everything was packed down below. These were the last things I had to collect.

I stepped over the log the strutting blue grouse had stood on to boom out his throat sacs and I dropped down from the ridgetop. The sun had been out and strong long enough that instead of slithering down loose mud my moccasins puffed up tan dust. Boone, as usual, charged down ahead of me, skipping the switchbacks, thrilled by the speed the drop gave her. Every so often she'd whirl around in a cloud of dirt and dust, just to make sure I was still coming along.

When I reached the bottom I dropped away from the trail and followed Indian Creek to my tent. Rader was there already, waiting to pick me up and take me out. I got into his station wagon and, instead of turning out, we drove down the road to Paradise. There was really only one thing to do with Boone.

The Texas bear hunters were still camped at Paradise. Rader pulled into their camp and stayed behind the wheel studying his fingernails while I got out with Boone. Three bear carcasses hung from the meat racks, skinned. A skinned bear looks eerily like a human being. I didn't know that until then.

I turned away from the bears as the women and their husbands came out of their tent. The woman infatuated with Boone dropped right down and started her petting. They were just mixing their happy hour and wanted to make an extra for me. I didn't have time, I said. I asked if they were still interested in my dog.

Of course she was interested, the woman said, looking up from Boone, if I really thought I could give her up.

I'd brought this up with them before, and I said again that I didn't have much choice.

The hunters lived on a five-thousand-acre ranch in Texas. Or fifteen thousand, or fifty thousand—I wasn't picking up everything they said. They told me Boone would have the run of the place, that she wouldn't be tied up there. I was in such a hurry to get this over with I didn't even think to get their address.

I shook hands all around, leaving Boone's rope leash in the hand of the woman who would take care of her now. I got back into the Deerslayer then and Rader started to drive toward the pass without saying anything. First thing we had to do was pull over for more incoming trucks.

I looked through the window at the tight, dark, wet looking walls of the Selway, and then down at the wild jumble of water. The river was growing in strength every day and my tiny salmon were in there somewhere, fighting to survive in the chaos.

When the road was clear for a moment we started to roll again, leaving Boone, my spring and my salmon behind. Although I'd come here simply to have a story of my own to tell, it was quite some time before I could think of anything to say.

EPILOGUE

After another summer lifeguarding at Lake Mead, I spent the following winter backpacking in New Zealand before returning to Missoula and graduating in wildlife biology. I was working as a river ranger on the Snake River four years later when my salmon fought their way back upstream from the Pacific, through the dams and the fishermen. Of the two and a half million eggs I'd guarded, fewer than twenty fish returned to Indian Creek.

AFTERWORD

For several years after that winter, I returned to the Selway as soon every spring and as late every fall as possible, caught up in my own personal migratory cycle. I was never around in the summers, first lifeguarding in the desert at Lake Mead, Nevada, then running the Snake River in the Tetons for the Park Service. But even if I had been around, I don't think I would have had much interest in seeing that place under the baking sun, the grasses turned brittle and scorched. And the trip over the pass in winter held little more for me. I'd done that already, the long slog on snowshoes, and this time, with no brother or father missing and overdue, there would be nothing driving me on.

Friends of mine, smoke jumpers for the Forest Service, told me of jumps they'd made back in the Selway. Even safe, out of the smoke and heat, they held the terrain in awe, the insane degree of the up and down. Some, after jumping from planes, had been taken out along the Magruder Corridor. "I saw your place. Where you spent that one winter. I told the other guys about it."

"Did it burn?"

"Close," they'd tell me, naming drainages and ridges I didn't know. I'd recognize them by sight, I guessed, but having been there alone, I'd never really needed names. Who would I have used them with?

The first fall after my winter on Indian Creek, I returned to school in Missoula. No, as I've sometimes been asked, I had not forgotten how to talk in my seven months of on-again, off-again isolation. But something had changed. My friends tell me it was more than just something. "Always carrying guns around? Doing whatever you wanted? Not bothering with anything as annoying as laws? Man, you were weirder than shit!"

I don't see it *quite* like that, but school was tough—all the rules, all the people. Only a week into the semester, I called Idaho and asked if the Indian Creek job was open again. A secretary in the Lewiston headquarters told me, "No, we've already got somebody lined up."

As it turned out, I met that somebody the next spring. Not a mountain man of legend, but a small, older, intensely silent man who completely ignored the sound of my truck pulling into the meadow, stopping and shutting off at the horse ramp, yards from his tent. He did finally stoop through the front flap in answer to my "Anybody home?" He took my information about preceding him the previous winter with a nod. I asked how his winter had gone. He said, "All right."

It'd been a much, much milder year, the pass open for months. Eventually I crowbarred out the news that he'd trapped all winter, running his lines on snow machine. The lack of snow had been a problem. He showed me his carcass pile: a rotting, pestilent mass impressively close, considering the smell, to the tent.

I asked how the salmon had done.

He shrugged.

When I said I was just going to poke around, take a look at things, he returned to his tent. I didn't get a look inside, see how he'd gone about organizing it. He didn't come out again when I fired up the truck. Maybe he'd left on some obscure business of his own. Maybe he was inside, staring at the water-stained canvas walls, the trapping season over, nothing to do. I don't know.

That first year back in Missoula after Indian Creek, I made it through one quarter. Then, leaping at a geology excursion, I enrolled in a few courses offered in New Zealand. Changing hemispheres, the year after living in my tent surrounded by snow, I missed winter altogether.

In New Zealand, I stuck it through the classes until we

stopped touring the islands, then I left the university group for a hitchhiking, backpacking expedition that kept me in the country until my visa was due to expire. I returned to Lake Mead and another summer of rescues, of 120-degree temperatures.

Then, finally, back to Missoula to finish it off. My education to that point had shown me little more than that I was not much interested in a career in Wildlife Biology, not that I had any ideas of what I *did* want to do. I stacked on the credits, knowing, as difficult as it had grown for me to toe any line, I'd have to graduate that year or never at all.

My last quarter that spring, I was stunned to discover I'd added up my credits incorrectly. Instead of reaching the absolute minimum required to graduate, I was still three credits shy of the magic number. I searched the catalog for anything offered at night, the only time I could fit another class.

I came across Introduction to Creative Writing, Tuesday and Thursday, 7–10. Pure, blind, dumb luck. The teacher was Bill Kittredge, more of the same luck.

We had one assignment: Write a six-page story with only two characters and one setting, and by the end of the six pages the characters must reach some resolution to a problem between them.

Imaginatively enough, I wrote about a man living in the mountains. In winter. Alone. His partner comes out to tell him he won't be joining him. Some resolution, I can't remember what, is reached. A shameful degree of mountain man taciturnity and surliness was involved, stolen right from Boone Caudill and A. B. Guthrie, no doubt.

But in writing those six pages, I *saw* the thick wool layers those two imaginary men wrapped themselves in, the tangle of clumsy stitching holding together the tear in a sheepskin mukluk, even how one of them picked at that heavy thread while listening to what he did not want to hear from his partner. I saw the leap and ebb of the campfire's flames, the shifting, hard-edged shadows against the snow, the dance of light on the ponderosa's jigsaw puzzle bark, and beyond those trees, the black nothingness of a snowy night far from anywhere. I felt the touch of cold when the man finally lifted his head to answer, exposing a bit of neck. I even felt the tightness in his throat, his disappointment, his not knowing what to say, only that it had to be something, anything to stop his partner's explanations and excuses.

In that writing, I was transported from the filthy chair in the ramshackle house I lived in with my college roommates. I was back out there. In the snow. In the mountains. I was, practically, back in Indian Creek. I had discovered the intensity of daydreaming with pen in hand.

And when the day came that Bill Kittredge read my story in class, the normally stupefyingly apathetic students came alive, arguing about my characters as if they were real people. Bill looked around the room and asked, "Who wrote this?"

The last thing I was going to do was admit it, but he picked me out, by my blush probably. "I don't know who you are, anything about your plans, but you could do this for a living."

After looking around at all the writers I knew, I began my park ranger career in the Tetons. (In my usual thorough, searching manner, I didn't know that Kittredge was himself a writer. I didn't even know that Missoula had a writing program, let alone one of the country's better ones). But though I was rafting the Snake River every day, the thrill of inventing those two people who came to a resolution in the snow and cold of my imagination did not ebb. The next winter, staying with my friends in another crumbling house, The Rancho Deluxe, but no longer going to school, I killed time between downtown excursions by flipping through my roommates' course catalogs.

Finding another night course in creative writing, Fiction 520 or something, I wound up sneaking in. At the end of the first night, as the other students headed for the door, the prof, Rick DeMarinis, signaled for me to meet him at the front of the room.

"You're not a grad student, are you?"

"Um, not exactly." I shook my head. I hadn't realized it was a graduate-level class.

"What's your name?"

I told him.

He looked at some sheet of paper, then at me. "Are you a student at all?"

I glanced away, surprised at being seen through so readily. I did the only thing I could think of. I grinned.

He smiled back, shaking his head. "You know, I've never had somebody try to sneak *into* one of my classes before."

The next night, asking the real students' permission, he let me stay for the quarter. At the end of my last story, he wrote a dead-on critique, listing my strengths and weaknesses, wrapping up by saying, "If you want it, you could have a career."

A career? In what? Making up imaginary friends?

I hitchhiked around the West, something that was becoming a winter tradition, going to see my sister near Galveston, my old cronies around Lake Mead. It was a way to fill the months between my seasonal work in Wyoming, and by spring I was back at the Tetons.

But my imaginary friends wouldn't leave me alone. I found I was getting up earlier and earlier, working on stories before starting my ranger shift. In winter, camped out in Missoula or in Great Falls with Rose, the woman who would kill me if I called her anything as mundane as a girlfriend, I wrote more stories. And even hitchhiking, I made myself up as a new character for every driver. Something had to give.

After buying a book called *The Novel and Short Story Writer's Marketplace*, I started to collect my first rejection notices. Over the years, they grew into the hundreds. (Now they've broken the thousand mark).

Then one story sold. *Louisiana Literature* paid me two free copies of the magazine my work appeared in, nearly the same wages I'd earned at Indian Creek.

I was suddenly a professional writer. Published and everything. I quit my job.

A couple of years later, a small California publisher, John
Daniel, took a chance and published a collection of my stories, *The
Tall Uncut*. In the author bio, that listing of all the odd jobs writers
take because they don't make diddly writing, my Indian Creek winter was summed up as "guarding two million salmon eggs for the
state of Idaho."

One of the review copies landed at *Outside Magazine*, and
somebody there took note. Instead of reviewing the book, they
called to ask, "What's this egg-guarding thing?"

I told them, and the editor asked if I'd consider writing a five-
part series for their winter issues. He named a price per piece that,
multiplied by five, exceeded my projected lifetime earnings as a
writer.

I sat down and wrote. Moving in to Indian Creek. Shooting
the moose. Searching for my dad and brother. Finding the bobcat.
And, finally, the icing-out of the river in the spring. I sent them
out.

A while later, a call. "Loved them! Loved them! But at the editorial board meeting, somebody pointed out that we don't do
series."

"But you said—"

"So, what we were wondering, what we'd like you to do is,
everybody really loved the spring, the ice thing. Could you write a
little intro, let everybody know what you were doing, why you
were there, and then do the ice thing? Still in two thousand
words?"

"Don't you think, without all the winter before it, that it
might lack the kind of impact it has now?"

"You can do it. What you've got now is terrific."

So, lackey that I am, I sat down and wrote a two-paragraph
introduction and iced-out the river. Crack, swoosh.

"Loved it! Loved it! But, at the editorial board meeting,

everybody kind of thought it didn't have the same impact it had before. Nobody could put their finger on it exactly, we all loved it, but . . ."

On the same day that that forlorn manila envelope returned, my huge payday up in smoke, John Daniel sent me an ad he'd found for the Sierra Club's annual nature writing award. Two thousand words, nonfiction, on the natural world. I took the ice-out from one envelope and put it in another.

A while later, I got a call. "You win!" They sent my prize—a pair of binoculars—and published the ice-out.

Then book publishers started calling. "Do you have more about that winter? A book?"

"Well, not a book exactly, but I've got these five pieces. . . ."

I sold the book before it was written, not having even guessed such a thing was possible.

But those five pieces, I thought, were the highlights. Now I had to come up with a couple hundred pages of filler.

Although I'd been telling stories about that winter for years and people, Rose in particular, had been urging me to write about it, I'd never been greatly tempted. Writing fiction is, to me, this big adventure: I don't know what will happen, and dropping into that unknown, with all the possibilities of discovery, is exactly what attracts me. But, with Indian Creek, I knew what happened— somehow, against all odds, the chucklehead survives. I didn't much look forward to the writing.

But twelve years had passed since that long, cold winter, and for the first time I pulled out the journals I'd kept in my futile attempt to keep my scholarship. I read them a week ahead of what I was writing about and found that there was still a sense of discovery. Certain things, the eclipse for example, had been sidelined in my mind, and reading the fifteen pages I'd written that same night, the dazzling darkness still sizzling in my mind, brought the day back with an immediacy I hadn't anticipated.

And as often happens, writing it all out, trying to find the con-

nective tissue that holds a story together, I discovered more about
that winter, much more than my previous simple view of having
accomplished something hard or even a bit bizarre, of having gathered a few good stories. When writing about finding the bobcat,
about how close I'd come to missing that whole strange occur-
rence, I realized I was reading the turning point of my entire winter—that what was good, and rare, and going to end, was not my
time in Missoula but my time at Indian Creek. Before working on
that chapter, I'd never known any such thing about myself.

With all the moving back and forth between Wyoming and
Montana, Great Falls and Missoula, the hitchhiking and story
writing, it had been years since I'd been back to the Selway. But I
didn't feel the need to visit in order to write the book. The place is
etched into me. So the first trip back I made was to do a National
Public Radio interview when the book came out. Washington,
D.C., likes sound in their pieces, and running water seemed a nat-
ural for this interview. But rather than simply running down to the
Clark Fork and doing it there, as I suggested, the interviewer,
William Marcus, wanted the real thing.

We met in Missoula and made the long drive down together.
By this time I'd been interviewed by TV weathermen, "morning
guys" on the radio, newspaper reporters. I'd learned it was rare to
talk with someone who'd heard of me before, but to find someone
who'd actually read any of my stories was truly freakish. But as we
drove into the Selway, stopping at the failing cabins at Slow Gulch
where my dad and brother had spent their long, long night, and
then at Magruder where I'd chased after them, William began to
notice things. "Is that the sign they knocked the snow off of?" he
asked, pointing at the sign for Kerlee Creek. I had to think about it
before nodding.

"Is this where you found the bobcat?"

I glanced up at the cliff, then over at him, suspiciously.
"You've read the book?"

Read it? He knew it better than I did.

We stayed all day. We got caught in a hailstorm (great sound!), walked up Indian Ridge a ways ("Is this where you sat that first evening, with Boone, wondering what you'd done?"), and he had me read that passage from the book. It was a strange, strange feeling, sitting up there again, reading about something that had happened long before I could have imagined this as a result.

As we drove back to Missoula, I asked about the technology, how he could take the hours and hours of tape he'd recorded and condense it to a six- or seven-minute interview. "I mean, what will I wind up saying?"

He smiled. "Whatever I want."

Several years and story collections later, I was on a book tour, reading in Boise. Afterward, a woman came up with a tattered copy of Indian Creek for me to sign, and told me that she (or her son or daughter or somebody—everything gets tangled at signings, and details are hard to recall) was planning on spending the millennium change, New Year's Day, at the Magruder Cabin. I'd inspired the idea, she said. Magruder had been added to the list of cabins the Forest Service rents out.

When I got home from that book tour, I called the West Fork Ranger Station, and eventually got a reservation for the next summer. This was not an easy task; somebody'd canceled.

Rose and I were married by then, with two young boys. We'd bought a house in Great Falls, and within days of moving in, my sister Ellen sent back the bobcat skin. It hangs on the wall in the basement guest bedroom. The boys sometimes go down there just to look at it, this wild thing in our staid old house. There was a phase they went through, about six months' worth, when I had to tell the story about the bobcat at bedtime every single night.

The entire ride in to the Selway that summer, at the least outcrop of rock, the slightest promise of cliff, the boys asked, "Is that where the deer jumped off because he wasn't watching where he was going when the bobcat was on his back?"

"No. Not yet. I'll tell you."

"Is that it?"

"Not yet."

We drove down the river, dodging around huge trucks working on the road—the daunting trail having been turned into something of a gravel superhighway—until at last I pulled over at Raven Creek, walked them back down the road, and pointed up.

They squinted against the bright sky, the dark rock. "Where's the snow?"

"Well, it's summer, there's no snow now."

"Where's the deer?"

"The deer? It's been dead for twenty years."

They turned to find good sticks, to throw rocks into the rapids.

We headed the last few miles to Indian Creek and walked over the tent site, then back into the trees, winding around the downed wood the boys couldn't step over. We found the food cache, still a depression in the ground. The path to the creek, my water trail, was intensely overgrown, and as I tried to pick a way the boys could follow, we heard a voice behind us, someone following us into the trees. I was in the lead and couldn't hear what was said. Our friends with us from Spokane, bringing up the rear, said, "What?"

The guy, a volunteer for the Forest Service it turned out, asked again, "Are you looking for Pete Fromm's tent site?"

I was ready to sidle back into the trees and vanish, as I had in the spring when the bear hunters started to appear.

Our friends laughed. "This *is* Pete Fromm!"

After talking to him, watching him leave, we wound our way back to the moose hanging pole. The boys made me lift them up so they could dangle down, just like a moose piece. They couldn't think of anything funnier. We walked along the old channel, still there, about as dilapidated as concrete and river rock can get. I pointed out the dry concrete lip where I used to chop ice.

Finally we headed back upstream to Magruder, and after getting around the flag person at the old stone bridge, we dropped down the last hill to the ranger station, the boys piling around me as I worked on the front door's combination. I thought of slipping through this door a step behind the wardens, scared to death, or piling in with Rader and Sponz, all of us laughing, or later, of staggering in with my snowshoes still on, the blackness of night tight around me, exhausted from my trip to the pass and back, looking for Dad and Paul.

I opened the door and the boys and our friends' daughter tumbled in, tearing through the rooms like dogs in a new spot, surveying every corner. I stood in the doorway. The old crank-up phone was missing. No more land-line wire threading through the trees.

The walls were paneled and bright. A propane stove sat where most cabins might have a wood stove. A thermostat sat perched on the wall. A thermostat. I creaked open the basement door. The hulking black mass of the wood furnace was gone. Upstairs the old bathtub had been replaced by a fiberglass shower stall.

The kids were already out of the house, over the buckrail, tearing through the long grass of the meadow toward the river. Shouting their names barely checked them, so I scrambled after. There were safety talks to give, warnings about the river, demonstrations of its swiftness, its bone-chilling cold, its stark beauty and sudden lethality.

At the buckrail beside the river, I gave orders. "No one, ever, will go past this fence unless I am with you, or Mom. Not ever."

"Why?"

"I'll show you. The water is super cold, and super fast, and—" I'd stepped up to the fence, watching the boys. I put my hand up on the top rail, my foot on the lower, and turning toward the river to see what I was doing, to keep from breaking my neck, I was stopped cold by the long, dark shapes firing across the jumble of current to the other side of the Selway.

Our four-year-old said, "Did you see the big fish what did swim away?"

Together, we scrambled onto the pack bridge and peered over the rail, me with a hand on both their collars. Salmon stretched the length of the eddy, jostling now and then, holding their positions.

Our six-year-old asked, "Are those your salmon, Dad?"

It was a second before I could say, "No, not mine. But they're the same kind. Chinooks."

"Maybe babies of yours."

I nodded. Maybe babies.

Though my fly rod was ridiculously light for the task, I worked the biggest, heaviest fly I had at the salmon until one had finally had enough and took an annoyed slash.

I'll spare you the hook and bullet, reel-smoking runs and all. It was a tired old fish, but even so, the boys whooped and hollered, following me down the bank until I could gravel him out. I let them get their shoes wet, so they could touch such a great thing.

They did, bent over it and studying. "How come you only catched tiny fish before?"

"This is not like other fish. This is a salmon. It came all the way from the ocean to here. A thousand miles. More than that."

I had the salmon by the tail, the hook out. "I'm going to let him go. Do you want another touch?"

Our four-year-old did. "Get your hand wet first!" our six-year-old instructed. They put their hands on his back, felt the surge, a dark flash up into the teeth of the river's charge, and then nothing. He was gone.

We stood up slowly and watched the water racing toward us, slick and smooth, and, suddenly, very empty.